About the Author

Larry Holme is a hotelier in Kent, England, whose passion for helping young people is witnessed in his continued commitment to the Army Cadet Force as a volunteer. He has also built schools in Peru and Kenya, actively taking on the work himself. With twenty-two years in business and twelve years working with young people to better their lives, he has also found time to start writing. With a degree in Hospitality Management and one in Leadership Management, Larry is currently studying for his third in Psychology in order to better support his family.

Straight Dad, Gay Dad

Larry Holme

Straight Dad, Gay Dad

Olympia Publishers
London

www.olympiapublishers.com
OLYMPIA PAPERBACK EDITION

A CIP catalogue record for this title is
available from the British Library.

ISBN: 978-1-80074-820-0

First Published in 2023

Olympia Publishers
Tallis House
2 Tallis Street
London
EC4Y 0AB

Printed in Great Britain

Dedication

For my rock, my conscience, and my muse – my husband.

Acknowledgements

If it wasn't for all the young people in my life that inspire and motivate me, this book would not have been written. My thanks to them especially. Thanks to my sister for telling me how bad the first version was and thanks to all the people who helped me get it published.

Intro

This book is not a 'how to' or in any way a 'guide to' when it comes to single sex couples parenting. I don't think I will ever really know how to be good parent. I'm bound to have a test creeping up round the corner on me that would prove I know absolutely nothing about what's about to happen. It's a learning curve that resembles more a frustrated child's doodle than a curve. I've read dozens of parenting books, fostering books, therapeutic manuals, and mental health papers. These are compulsory reading lists, suggested reading lists, and those that just interested me. All of it was interesting, none of it prepared me completely for the challenges that lay ahead. None of them were a 'how to' or a 'guide to' either. Perhaps my opening disclaimer is also at the beginning of every other parenting book. I will need to look out for it. There are still a thousand unanswered questions that rely on my experience to tell me that truth, as you really don't know until it happens. As I read these books, I couldn't help but think how helpful they would be to any hopeful parent, professional or natural. A small government initiative that would see book tokens awarded to budding parents for them to get a selection of parenting books for free would certainly assist many challenges of the modern parent and child relationship. It would also help parents discuss the strategies they want to take as parents with each other. Most of our arguments with each other stem from the disagreements on how to handle a particular situation. The truth is that, in our disagreements, we end up with the very best solution for the child in question. It's the process of putting across your point and explaining why you think you are right that creates an agreed outcome that is usually the best. The trick is not to do it in front of the child, we have learnt.

One of my favourite reads on the 'suggested list' for adoption was *Becoming Dads by Pablo Fernandez, published by CoramBAAF Adoption and Fostering Academy*. I found it incredibly helpful. He journalled his story in a diary format, from the inception of the idea to the completed mission. It is a detailed story about gay adoption in 2009, which I briefly experienced myself. I take a lot of inspiration from his book. It's honest, heartfelt, revealing, and informative. My journey, although similar, ends up very differently despite the challenges along the way in the same category of two males fighting through the 'system'. I saw a lot of their own emotional journey mirrored in my own and I guess that reading their journey compelled me to narrate my own because of the simple fact that, although in the same demographic of human, our journeys and paths differ in many ways following the same dream. I guess that, like so many other gay couples out there, my journey will differ from theirs but, by reading about ours, it will only give some form of comfort that it's a journey shared by many. It may not be quite as special or pioneering as Pablo Fernandez and his Daily Mail front pager. It is, however, special to me and I hope that it relates to many other parents, single sex couples, single parents, non-binary or good old-fashioned man and woman.

This book is a chronicle of a journey documented for the benefit of others, or at the very least your enjoyment. It's not intended to be funny, although sometimes might be. It's also a bit of an emotional rollercoaster. Such is the rollercoaster of life, mine just happens to include single sex relationships and children. Many years ago, those two things were not permitted in the same sentence. To this day, it's a little taboo for many. The names of those children and some adults within my story have been changed to protect their identity but they are all real people. The real lives described in these pages may help others to understand the process of applying to care for a child that is not biologically yours as a single sex couple. It describes some of the experiences you may go through – we certainly did. It doesn't cover everything, how can it? Your journey, if you are embarking on one, will definitely have challenges, most definitely will be mentally exhausting, and may have some similarities to our own journey. I have tried to be as factually correct as possible but I'm pretty sure some of the quotations may not be perfect. It's certainly difficult to get a Gloucester accent into some of the comments, but I have tried. The colloquial language of youth is also best left to them. My translations certainly make more sense to me and probably to you.

Our current rather unusual family is made up of misfits and strays and is just perfect in our eyes. From the deaf and blind rescue dog to the nominated and background-checked neighbours, everyone has a part to play in our crazy life looking after those in need. We wouldn't change it for the world, the reward is ten times the pain. The cathartic process of writing down how we got here is enjoyable, emotional, and surprising in some moments too. The cathartic process of completing Form F (more on that later) was also enjoyable, emotional, and surprising. The views and opinions expressed in this book are solely mine and do not reflect the opinions of any governing body or charity. They probably don't reflect the views of my husband either. We do have completely different parenting styles, that's for sure. It's probably what makes us better parents because of it. Some of those heated debates I mentioned earlier included things like the right language to use around removing the Xbox but, as with life, there are bigger things to worry about and we never go to bed in disagreement. Is it remove the Xbox, confiscate the Xbox, ban it, put it in timeout, or smash it with a hammer? Seriously, all of these crossed our minds. We continuously challenge each other's decisions and question what's right and wrong. Sometimes to the detriment of our sanity and, if it were not for our strength of relationship in the first place, I honestly believe that adding these little terrors to our life may well have put a bigger strain on our marriage than we could have possibly coped with. It didn't and we haven't.

Robin, my husband, is definitely the rules guy. He sets the boundaries, protects them, and enforces them with strict enthusiasm. I play the fool, the joker, and the 'fun one'. I kick around the football, play nerf wars, pretend to be in the secret service (this one is partly from my encouragement), you know, the usual stuff. It's funny because we both thought that it would be the other way round. I've spent twelve years in the Army Cadet Force instilling military discipline into teenage girls and boys. Teaching them the values and standards of the military whilst maintaining strict respect and discipline.

As an officer, I would walk into a room and the room would need to come to attention. That certainly does not happen at home, I can assure you. Discussing parenting with some of my military friends, they too fail to maintain the standards of the military at home as well as at work. It should be natural for me to carry that over to my personal life, but the opposite happens. You would have thought that perhaps the roles were natural. My friends certainly expected me to the be grumpy Daddy and Robin to the big soft cuddly one. We didn't aim for those roles or to shoehorn our personalities into them, they just manifested in them. I think that, because Robin is the stay-at-home dad, he has to deal with the tantrums, tiredness, hanger, and a plethora of other youth and growth mental developments so he has to lay on the rules thick. I, on the other hand, share pancake tossing competitions and good night stories – easy in comparison.

In our usual private daily lives, Robin is the crazy one, always the life of any gathering. The entertaining one with the anecdotes and stories to hold a room. He is naturally extroverted and has been his whole life. Even when he came down with a rather serious case of anxiety, he managed to hold onto his extroverted approach to making and keeping our circle of friends. I, on the other hand, am naturally introverted. An unusual but not unheard-of personality in my main chosen industry to pay the bills, which is hospitality. I have worked in restaurants, nightclubs, bars, pubs, and hotels my entire career. At work, I am a showman. I have to work hard on acting my extroverted approach to the guest experience. I happen to be very good at this and ensuring my guests get the very best welcome, experience, and therefore memory is my skill. Even when things are tough, I turn on the 'plappy' side (play happy). I can do it on a switch and, believe me, sometimes it's hard but I do it, it's my job. At home, I am opposite – I switch off my hospitality smile and turn to reading the news, cooking, or mowing the lawn. All blissful pastimes in comparison to the relative fast pace of a Sunday afternoon pub kitchen. We have morphed into opposite versions of ourselves when it comes to parenting. It's all very confusing to us both still today. Should you be able to understand it, we will need you to write to us and explain it.

We have been through quite a few challenges, both mentally and physically. The emotional turmoil of mental health issues, the death of family and loved ones, the break ups, the job losses, and the financial crashes. All part of everyday life which many of you would have experienced yourself and, I'm sure, can empathise with. If, perhaps, you have been lucky enough to avoid any type of emotional or physical adversity, then becoming a parent to a non-biological child may not be the best introduction to the world of stress and challenge. Managing a team of room service waiters in a five-star hotel who only want to smoke, gossip, and flirt with pretty much everyone is the sort of training I'm talking about. It's marginally similar to looking after teenagers and, without the former, the latter is going to be so much harder. No amount of experience can prepare you for your first placement of a child in your home, but herding drag queens on a Saturday night in Soho is still good practice.

When it comes to bringing children into the mix of your life whose backgrounds are so desperately troubled, much more so than our own, it puts our own lives in perspective. Especially in a single sex couple where we're already on the back foot or defensive position. That new perspective helped us get over our own challenges and immerse ourselves in helping young people become better versions of themselves in a safe and happy environment. That's all we wanted to do – help young people. We knew that was our calling in life. It wasn't to procreate – our family genes would not continue with us. Surrogacy was beyond our financial means and felt all a little bit weird to us. Our paternal feelings have always superseded our maternal feelings. Our discussions about the subject were brief and in agreement. We decided to leave that to our brothers and sisters, who are all doing a fantastic job of creating life, plenty of it. We have seventeen nephews and nieces between us, two great nieces, and three godchildren. We believe our calling in life is to help at least one of the approximately one hundred thousand children in care currently in the United Kingdom.

1

1988 – Natural Dads

It started in 1988 when I realised some things about myself. The most interesting of which was that I was gay. To be precise, it was the twenty-fourth of May 1988 when I realised. I know this because it was the public reaction to Section 28, twelve days after my eighth birthday, that made me realise who I was. My mother read the *Daily Mail*, more out of routine than anything, and their viewpoint being mostly right-wing, you can imagine how it felt to be picking up the odd copy of the paper to read its gripping headlines. Not that my mother was right-wing at all. In honesty, totally the opposite, but the newspaper was always there. The reporting on Section 28 and the mandate itself was written with such hatred and authorised by, as it turns out, plenty of homosexual members of parliament. Work that out! The messed-up world of politics in the '80s, created something by design that was supposed to deter the incorrect theory that talking about gays made everyone gay.

Talking about not talking about it actually made me realise I was gay and that it was okay. Completely the opposite desired outcome of Section 28. How did I know it was okay? Well, several fat old queens in wigs were saying it wasn't, that was enough for me to understand that it was. I also realised at that point that, no matter what, I did not want to get into politics.

At eight, I know I was gay. I was also very 'straight' socially. Confusing times, when the only gay icons of the day were in Carry On movies or wore drag. The idea that we had Dame Edna or Kenneth Williams as our go to stereotypes to look up to was concerning for many, especially me. I was not them at all. In fact, I was completely opposite to these characters. I, on the other hand, was a boy who climbed trees, rode bikes, played rugby, and I even chased girls. I did all the normal things that any young man would do in the pre-millennial time before social media and online gaming. As I grew up, I had several girlfriends, often alongside 'fancying' boys. I remember watching 'Flight of the Navigator' and fancying the young male actor, Joey Cramer, at the same time being jealous that he got to fly a spaceship. 'Saved by the Bell' was one of my favourite programmes, best remembered for Zack Morris, played by Mark-Pail Gosselaar, and his pal, Mario. Sitting, watching it with my family, hoping they didn't notice how my attention would prick up if a sports scene appeared. Would they think it's my love of American football as opposed to the crop top training fatigues?

As a young man with few people to role model for me, if any, I thought I was the only one in the world who felt like this. It was very lonely feeling emotional about boys while conforming to publicly feeling emotional about girls. I finally found a young pen pal from New Zealand who was my age and sexuality, eleven thousand five hundred miles away. The relationship didn't last long as written mail was easily and often intercepted by adults. One silver lining, it turns out that, at thirteen, it doesn't matter who you're kissing, the reaction down below is the same. I also managed to steal a few kisses from my 'straight' friends at school. Boarding school inherently and unintentionally encourages situational homosexuality. Anyone who denies it – well, you know. I made some mistakes too – stealing a kiss from a friend as I hoped he would kiss me back has cost me dearly. I don't regret much in my life but misinterpreting some of those events I regularly wish hadn't happened. I didn't, however, know what else to do and although damaging to my friendships, I hope it was not damaging to my friends.

The importance of starting a family was always obvious to me. I knew I had it in me to be a good dad. I was naturally caring, thoughtful, and a leader. I would take charge and, before I even knew what the term even was, servant leadership came naturally to me. I was awarded 'Camp Butler' at my end of year awards aged twelve for my efforts on the leavers camping trip to serve tea and biscuits to the adults on an overturned saucepan lid. I giggled to myself as I was the only one who thought describing me as camp was funny. Probably the word 'butt' too. I was naturally protective over young kids in the school. I developed ahead of most of the other boys, so was bigger and stronger than most. Instead of using it to my advantage by asserting myself, I would use it to protect the younger kids in the school. It has always felt to me that caring for other people is in my nature. A wing to shield and protect would be available to anyone who needed it. I'm pretty sure that my parents were already pigeon-holing me for a career in the police or medical profession. Robin too. In fact, his whole family are naturally caring people. Probably one of the best reasons we get along so well. That ability to give yourself, your time, and your money for the benefit of others without thinking twice about the lack of quality you may get yourself.

Even at such a young age, I had a very clear understanding of what it meant to be a dad. People underestimate the mind of an eight-year-old but, in one sense, its underdeveloped state ensures one thing for sure, it's not yet polluted by external social factors. Which is why I worry about the easy access to social media on today's young people. It is the natural demand for social acceptance and shaming those without it that concerns me the most. Add into this the cultural need for instant fame, likes, and instant approval from your friends. Feeding off the fake photo filters to make you look thinner, smoother, or more muscular while you relish in their jealousy. The greatest threat to all is those dreaded social apps that are, by design, so dangerous and actually encourage the sharing and timed deleting of pictures to each other. There is only one real reason kids love this so much, so they share what we did behind the bike sheds. Kids will be kids but now, once it's on the internet, it's there for ever. It scares me still. In contrast, I had a very happy childhood and upbringing without the need to post it online. There is a funny generational post I read recently about how someone fell over and grazed their knee skateboarding in 1988 but only now had the ability to post on Facebook twenty years later to tell everyone. We didn't need affirmation that my wound was newsworthy, required sympathy, and my toughness was likened to a Greek God, obviously. As a child, I wanted for nothing, and my parents provided me a very safe and fun upbringing.

The influence of television at the time was more innuendo and good clean fun. The children's programme, 'Rainbow', had a rather dysfunctional family made up of a man, a bear, a cheeky teenager, and a gay Pink Hippo. It's a wonder I grew up properly at all. Social media and its evils didn't exist. My pen pal in New Zealand was my closest ally and we only spoke twice. That was as close as I got to knowing another gay person my age until I left for university. We came up with elaborate ways we could be together, such an imagination. I'd never met him and shared only two letters but that didn't stop us. It was nervous enough having to be questioned by my father as he collected the international letters and presented them to me with one eyebrow higher than the other.

Those fun, safe days of my youth were spent growing up on a farm or at boarding school, those were the two places I spent my time. At school, I spent most of my time questioning the world's place for me in a place that was designed to steer young people to their place in the world. Sex education was all about men and women having intercourse to make babies. Perhaps it got a bit interesting around the subject of foreplay as a prerequisite for healthy intercourse, that's about as exciting as it got. In Religious Studies (my favourite teacher, least favourite subject), we talked about how men and women play an important union of two people around the world. Great – nothing on Ancient Greek same sex relationships or the modern rise of homosexuality and how, even though institutionalised by the Church, it is denied at every level. Those are the subjects I really wanted to challenge. At home on the farm, I spent most of my free time running around the woods pretending I was Rambo and waiting for my Spectrum ZX to load up Donkey Kong. I would spend hours and hours in make-believe worlds making up stories. So much fun being a special agent battling the world's evil. I still do that now. Hope it never stops.

There's plenty of discussion about the development of a young person's brain during training to become a professional parent. Particularly, in the mental health training element, you discuss the science behind the totally wild behaviour and decision making of young people. Also, the negative effects a poor upbringing has on their neurological development. At age eight, dopamine has not yet developed in the brain, in large quantities at least. Therefore, decision making is made mainly by the limbic system as the neocortex is still in the distant future of developmental stages. The limbic system is the fight or flight decision maker, often referred to as the reptilian element of our brain. Even reptiles understand fight or flight. Why is this important? Well, the design of a developing brain in young people is so very important in the current social climate. We are understanding more and more the stresses on youth and are openly discussing mental health in youth especially. We now understand what happens during adolescence and the challenges for teenagers, the developing mental state, and how fragile it is. When considering taking on a child in care, you are reminded of this constantly. Either from your family and peers or by the professionals themselves about the 'damage' some of these kids can have. What you learn very quickly is that most of this 'damage' is learned behaviour. The great thing about learned behaviour is that it can be 'un-learned'. There is a video on YouTube that explains this brilliantly, analogising a fist as a brain. The video, by Dr Russ Harris, explains the theories of Dr Dan Siegel in such a simple format. It's a format that even young people can understand so helps to explain it – or at least you can easily relay the theory to them if they're against a formal meeting. I have had to use this several times when explaining why they can't do something and that I am here to be their 'neocortex' – the rationalisation part of our brains – for the foreseeable future.

Despite my undeveloped grey matter, I knew one thing clearly, I was never going to procreate in the normal sense. Playing enough games of 'mummies and daddies' with my girlfriends developed that acknowledgement quite clearly. No chance was I going to ever put my thingy in that thingy. I had an older brother, he had magazines. It wasn't difficult to work out what to do. That realisation of not being able to procreate and therefore build my own family lineage was clear to me from that day. I also knew, however, that there were other ways to have a family. At eight, the details were a little fuzzy, but I had an aunt who was adopted so it wasn't totally alien to me. It didn't necessarily mean that I had to procreate to get any of those things. I understood parenting was about providing a safe environment for a child. Giving that child safety, security, and love when they needed it most. Putting a plaster on a grazed knee (prepped with TCP in my days) or educating them on right from wrong. Parenting didn't necessarily mean fertilising eggs and sharing DNA. I use some of these analogies with the children I share my time with now. I'm the guy who picks you up when you fall over, I'm the guy who wipes away your tears and tells you that you're going to be okay. I'll be the guy cheering you on at every major decision in your life, now and for ever, if that's what you need. That is what a parent is.

It was my parents' divorce in 1992 that helped me to understand the values I put under the heading of family. These values, although at a basic understanding from the age of eight, required a certain amount of cementing in reality to become proper values as opposed to a vague understanding. It was at this time that I had difficulty understanding what divorce meant, too. It was a fairly new term in the early '90s, although gaining popularity. I was one of the 'divorced parents' kids. Much like the 'ADHD kids' nowadays, I was made excuses for. I would often overhear, 'His behaviour must be to do with what's happening at home.' As if having divorced parents must be the reason, not the fact I was struggling with my sexuality, or the strains of moving school, or the fact I wasn't very popular, or any other number of challenges every child faces on a daily basis. My behaviour was pretty bad as a kid. I got up to all kinds of mischief and the teachers would always ask what home life was like, trying to find a reason as to why I was acting out of sorts from my peers. I went to a special school sponsored by the military. The RAF Benevolent Fund was sponsoring a school for the kids of servicemen and women. Therefore, it wasn't unusual for kids who played up to have excuses made of being from a military family without consistency of a dwelling or of a parent who had lost their life. So, the school was used to making these assumptions about the divorced kids, too.

I wanted to jump out of my skin, scream from the top of my lungs, and tell them all the truth. 'I'm a big fat queer, a faggot, a pansy', the only words I knew to describe myself. I was screaming in my head. Don't get me wrong, I was also pretty angry at my dad for treating my mum with so much disrespect, but that wasn't all my troubles. There was so much more to it. Society would shame homosexuals publicly, in the press, in the media. Gay characters on television would be stereotyped in such an awful way. Gary Glitter was demonised, quite rightly, for his awful paedophilic behaviour, but him being a celebrity and gay exaggerated the report. It was as if homosexuals were all sexual deviants. This encouraged the general public view that all gay people were sexually deviant, and without any healthy role models, who was to argue with them. How on earth would I ever be able to come out in a positive way? Did I even want to? Don't forget, I still thought I was the only one like this (apart from my mate in New Zealand). Despite the odd sexual experimentation with both boys and girls, none of the boys would admit the word 'gay' as a thing. As it turns out, none of them were actually gay later in life. It was just fooling around. As if life wasn't confusing enough, this only served to confuse me even more!

The feeling of being the only one was probably the most challenging of my emotions – loneliness. I couldn't rely on the modern benefits of social media and instant news reporting. I couldn't google what being gay was because it would take you to a medical centre for fixing gay people or an article on Michael Jackson. The closest thing I got was the Encyclopaedia Britannica male anatomy charts. The definition of a homosexual wasn't even included in the 1982 print and still its current online definition is shrouded in homophobic context. It talks mostly about how it 'started' and how Sigmund Freud characterised it as a result of conflicts of psychosexual development, including identification with the parent of the opposite sex. Laughable how I apparently identify with my mother more than my father. This couldn't be further from the truth, much to my own disappointment more than anything else.

In my own mind, I created my own set of values around family, love, and sharing my life with another human. These particular values reflected my interpretation of what family meant – loyalty, unconditional love, generosity, and togetherness. Those were instilled into me by my mother and siblings as we grew up. We fought like all siblings do, but we also shared family values that made us inseparable. To this day, we still argue but remain a relatively close unit.

My father demonstrated that he could not execute all the values that my siblings and I had. At the time, I thought my parents' values were make babies, make money, and buy a big house. Perhaps I'm confusing values and goals here. Perhaps I'm also confusing my father's goals with my mother's, which I'm certain are more in line with mine. As you can imagine, it was a very upsetting and a very dramatic time for a young man who had his own battles to deal with, which had now been overshadowed by an even bigger family drama. How dare they steal my limelight!

I have since come to terms with both tragedies, as I saw them, of my life. Since my father passed away in 2016, my disgust of his actions as a father passed away with him. Society is also not that angry with me for being homosexual and, surprise, surprise, I'm not the only one. This is not a coming out story, so I will spare you the details. In summary, everything was a lot less dramatic than I imagined.

2

2008 – Our First Attempt

I think I have to mention here that I've stopped caring what people think of me. Perhaps it's the processes I've been subject to that has hardened me emotionally. Perhaps it's just the fact I'm now a parent, so embarrassing young people is now a right of my employment and should be embraced. Getting old gives you a sense of right to be embarrassing and to not care what anyone thinks of you. Maybe it's both. Robin and I have been subjected to a lot of what could be misunderstood as interrogation in the process of becoming parents. It certainly felt like it sometimes, although all necessary. This level of questioning and interviewing by so many child care professionals has led to me having to self-evaluate on a number of occasions, whilst simultaneously being evaluated by others. We will go through many of these later in the book, but it has hardened me. Perhaps it removed a lot of the emotion from how I act around other people now. I used to want to impress my personality onto people in the first instance and ensure people liked me. I was always aiming to please and, in turn, be pleased by knowing people like me. I would be devastated if people didn't like me, what was wrong with me? In hindsight, that first impression should be natural, not contrived or strained, which I believe it may have been. This desire to impress and be liked was experienced first-hand at our first attempt to become gay adoptive parents.

Fast forward twenty years from the eight-year-old confused little boy on a mission. The older version of me had gone through some troubled times as a teenager, in and out of university, travelled much of the world, and was now engaged to the love of my life. My teenage years are another book in itself, but then so is everybody's. It was 2008 and we were living in Kingston-upon-Thames, both working good jobs – our thoughts turned to babies.

We had just returned from Spain from a four-year stint running a business on the Costa del Sol. I'd also managed to publicly advertise that on Gordon Ramsay's Kitchen Nightmares for Channel 4. In those days, people still watched normal television as YouTube had only been invented in the same month. Ten point one million viewers tuned in live, and I shudder to think now how many have 'caught up' watching it on demand. Millions more. Appearing on the show was actually a genius business decision and we went from impending closure to four successful trading years, hampered only by the 2008 recession and financial crash. My main customers were expats and their disposable income fell by forty per cent overnight, so did my business. Gordon, in reality, is actually a lovely caring man, not his television persona. That said, his alter ego is great for making tense, watchable programmes. We were attracted to Spain by the three hundred and twenty days of sunshine a year, property at half the price of the United Kingdom, and, at that stage, enjoying European free movement and employment rights. We had a beautiful big restaurant one hundred metres from the beach front. As I said, four great trading years with Gordon's help; unfortunately impacted greatly by the financial crash that affected so much of the world in 2008. I could see year four falling into the same financial challenges as year one and I did not want to experience that again. Our landlord was a corrupt local mayor who, not long after we left, was arrested for property fraud. So, quite glad we got out when we could. The pressure of being an immigrant making a success of a life in Spain was too much. We moved back to London. It wouldn't take us long to get back on our feet and, before you know it, we were in a position to start looking at our UK version of our dream life. In writing down what it would look like, it made the goals more digestible than just talking about them. I think I was reading Stephen Covey's 'The seven habits of highly effective people' when I discovered I needed to do this. I highly recommend it as a book for life goals, not necessarily for business excellence. If you can't, won't, or just don't want to, I still suggest you reach out and write down a list of things that are important to you. Then under each heading, write down what you are good at in that category and what you are not very good at. It may be that you are a leader in the community and do something for the greater good on a daily basis, but do you stop and help the elderly up the stairs with their bags?

My four goals:

One. Work – be the best I can be, enjoy what I do, and be respected by my peers.

Two. Community – be a positive force in the community, supporting and helping others.

Three. Family – be supportive, helpful, and loyal to family.

Four. Personal – be healthy in body and in mind.

We were good, but everything seemed to be missing a piece of the puzzle. We could easily evaluate each of the above points and I have below. It was the missing piece that we failed to work out what exactly it was. Perhaps in the journey to calculate the pillars of our future, we would find our missing piece.

We were happy in WORK, both doing things we loved with plenty of friends to share our success. I was working for Jamie Oliver in his new restaurant empire. Back then, it was the hottest high street restaurant opening in the industry and we were opening them at a rapid rate. I was self-appointed in charge of the bars for the group and relished the responsibility. Robin was working for another high street restaurant group. Being both in hospitality, we were like ships in the night sometimes and rarely saw each other, but we were busy and happy, our chosen industry being socially a lot of fun as opposed to its reputation for the opposite. We made many friends along the way, most of whom are straight. We didn't tend to hang out at gay clubs or socialise. We found the gay scene a bit much for us when we moved back from Spain. It seemed strange not to associate ourselves with the demographic that fought for our social acceptance, but it can be a little overbearing. The last thing we wanted was to fall into the traps of being in a promiscuous relationship that was famed in those circles at that time. The modern approach is a lot of more accepting and we don't have to hang around in underground clubs any more. We're actually allowed to hold hands in public now, which I assure you was not always the case even as recent as 2008.

My commitments to COMMUNITY translated into a role that I had always aspired to do. I was working with the Army Cadet Force as an adult volunteer. The military had always been a draw for me, but I never fully committed. Perhaps it was the fact that I didn't think I was 'allowed' to be gay in the Army. There was an old unwritten rule called 'don't ask, don't tell'.

Before 2000, it was actually illegal to be a member of the armed services and gay. At the age of nineteen, that's exactly when I wanted to enrol and didn't. In 2010, the US military repealed their official act of 'don't ask, don't tell'. Around the same time, the UK military followed suit but it was never an official written rule. It was unofficially repealed but took a while longer for people to get used to it. Too old now to sign up, I settled for and into a military role of helping young people in their journey in life. To help them achieve their potential through the values and standards of the military by being that role model. It was my way of doing something that I couldn't do when I was younger. I could achieve my potential within the military that I was never allowed to do before. It was very rewarding for me. As someone who hadn't managed to achieve my own potential at school, it was really helpful to me to help others achieve theirs. With plenty of experience of the Army Cadets at school, it felt right to me that this was my way of giving back to the community in the best way I knew how whilst following my own dreams.

In FAMILY, my sister had just given birth to her first child. I was aptly named 'Fairy God Father', which I found both hilarious and fitting. It was also one step closer to becoming a father of some sorts. Being a godfather is quite different, however. Duties mainly involved loading the kids up with sugar, loosening items of clothing, and handing them back madly in love with you but soon to let loose on their real parents with the inevitable sugar crash moments later. I have managed to be godfather to three beautiful little nippers. I'm so lucky to have been invited to be a part of young people's life from birth and can't wait to continue to uphold the title of those roles with the enthusiasm and ownership expected. This, accompanied with my duties as son, brother to another, and then uncle to fifteen nephews and nieces from my partner's side, we were more than covering the 'family' commitments expected.

PERSONAL contentment, I was over the social shock from Spain. Being a business owner for four years, featuring on the popular television programme 'Gordon Ramsay Kitchen Nightmares' was a very public thrashing. It changed me as an operator and the relative success we enjoyed off the back of the fame was exciting. The move to a junior manager position with Jamie's Italian was a difficult transition but I tried incredibly hard to make it work. Many people suffer from a form of mental illness nowadays, so I don't feel I was any different to anyone else struggling with self-worth. I think mine was a short spate of depression, I was in a very low place, but my partner, Robin, my patient mother, and my dog, Millie, helped pull me back from those dark days and got me back to full strength. I was stronger for it, mentally and physically. I embraced failure as much as success, knowing how it makes me who I am. You can never really fail in life if you learn from your lessons. I could only have recovered so quickly by embracing the support that was around me and knowing that I have people I loved caring for me. My partner, too, was the happiest we've been, getting all our ducks in a row so to speak. Leaving Spain and returning to the grey skies of London felt like a backwards step but, in time, we realised it was really the best thing for our relationship. No relationship is as strong as one that has been tested.

What was it about that missing piece that confused us so? We had achieved many of our goals at a fairly young age. We hadn't quite got on the housing ladder, a common curse of the millennials. Described more as a crisis nowadays, the amount of thirty to forty somethings who consider their lives will always be spent in rented accommodation grows by the minute. We were one of those people. The thing was, we knew that we would make good parents as we had so much experience with young people under our belt. We were confident that, although still young – thirty and twenty-five – we were ready. Despite the house, we had calculated that, financially, my income would still support us and a new little one. Robin would be stay-at-home dad and we could still save for a house in the future. We wanted to be parents. It was our missing link.

I have a spreadsheet for everything. My work is managed predominantly in cost analysis and profit margins so, financially, I had calculated we could afford to start a family. I was approaching it like a work project. My husband will vouch for you that I once did a spreadsheet and cost analysis on his spending habits. I wanted to show the difference in how we approached our life with incomings and outgoings. If we were a restaurant, we'd be bankrupt was possibly the analogy I used. It didn't go down well. I'm not allowed to communicate in spreadsheets at home again. However, my attempt at creating a fiscal strength portfolio for family planning went down a lot better and we were both confident we could make this work. We knew we wanted kids. We had two good jobs and a big enough house in a London borough. Lots of kids needed homes and we knew we would be awesome dads.

It was early 2010 when we plucked up the courage and enthusiasm to approach a charity who advertised as being specialists in placing single parent adoption and gay adoption. They were TACT, the UK's largest fostering and adoption agency according to their advertising. Even today, their website proudly demonstrates a focus on LGBT community, sponsoring the LGBT Adoption week, and proudly displaying their success stories online. As it turned out at the time we applied, they had placed very few gay couples and were more likely to have single gay men as single adopters. I guess this was the norm at that point. We were categorised as 'hard to place with'. There was obviously still a great deal of stigma attached to placing a child with gay adoptive parents. The 2002 Adoption and Children Act enabled unmarried couples to adopt (when it finally came into legislation in 2005). So, the recent changes were still very much a hot topic.

In 2007, the sexual orientation regulations act confirmed the right of gay couples. However, this was strongly disputed by the Catholic church charities, and it took two attempts to get it through the House of Lords before being enacted (probably the same old queens in wigs from the '80s). It wasn't until 2009 that Scotland followed suit; the Catholics finally conceded in 2010. The whole single sex adoption topic was very much in the press. A Gay couple not long before us had managed to get on the front page in the Daily Mail, being questioned for their suitability. All homosexuals are sexual deviants, obviously. It did make us feel inferior and not particularly very confident in the whole process. Not that we listened too much to the thoughts of the Daily Mail, but it does reflect a portion of the demographics in the UK and that worried us. Especially if our school is inhabited by those Daily Mail readers in the catchment area.

Fitting in with the mums is every parents' fear, not just gay dads. We didn't want to have the lives of potential children in our care plastered all over the tabloids.

The application process was rigorous. The form-filling initially would be followed up by an interview at one of their satellite offices. I had taken a day off work and met Robin outside their office in Walton, I believe, or some other obscure South London suburb. We were so nervous; this was the biggest commitment we had made together and felt nerve-worthy. The initial interview was successful, and they confirmed that they would like to progress the application further. This was amazing news. In our minds, this was the first and hardest step to take. We'd been accepted. The excitement, I think, spilled over to the work place, which spilled over to after work drinks, but who cared. We were too excited to hold it in and made the fatal mistake of just telling everyone. It's similar to not telling people you're pregnant until the second trimester, just in case. My advice is don't get too excited too early and don't tell everyone.

The all-important background checks had come back clear and our financial history investigations were also good. We weren't in debt, had good credit rating scores, and weren't serial murderers. These are all key attributes to becoming a parent. The first home visit came, and we were cleaning the house like never before. We had flat mates at the time, so had to hide them, too, until the supervisor had been and gone. The toilet got an extra level of scrubbing because, like me, I was sure she would judge anyone on the cleanliness of the toilet, and possibly only the toilet. She met my rather grumpy Spanish rescue dog who took an instant dislike to her. Not the best of starts, but we dismissed it as guarding the house and being a great protector of the family. The questions were intrusive, as always, and deeply personal. She asked us about our previous partners, sexual health, how much alcohol we consume, and a long list of other questions – some of which we thought were completely unnecessary and others that made us think hard about the decisions we were making. It was a pleasant enough exchange of words and, as she left, she took the obligatory visit to the bathroom to probably wipe a white glove under the bowl.

Two weeks later, we got the call to come back in for a final stage two assessment meeting.

One. You're too young.

Two. You don't have a stable dwelling.

Three. Call us in eighteen months.

They didn't put it in writing. It was probably for fear of legal ramification. We were just notified in a meeting at the end of the stage two assessment, that's all we knew. Robin was a little confused how questions on our sexual health had impacted on the decision that we were too young and didn't have a stable dwelling. These two quite specific reasons could have and should have been brought to our attention at the application stage, surely. We quietly accepted our news and left.

I wasn't aware there was an age limit on adoption and, being in my thirty-first year at the time, I presumed being too young was a bit of an excuse. Stable dwelling? Together, we were earning over fifty thousand pounds per annum, but it was the fact we had a private landlord who could legally end our contract at any time that was the issue. In all honesty, we left that meeting thinking that actually they were coming up with excuses because we were two guys. Such a deflating mixture of emotions, including anger and frustration. I only wished now that they had spent more time with us. They could have explained it better, reassured us more. To go through all the process only to be told at the end something that, to me, would have been clear from the start was very disheartening. I still believe now that the reason was that it was more difficult to complete a placement with a gay male couple in rented accommodation. So, in essence, they couldn't be bothered. Ironically, if we were in council housing, it would probably have been much easier.

We started to make up our own reasons, too. Perhaps we weren't good potential parents after all. So, why wasn't there a yes or no question saying, 'do you live in your own property or council accommodation?' It seemed that, without either of those reassurances, you won't get past stage one. The reason they are so coy about it is that there are serious legal ramifications stopping someone adopting because they are in private rented accommodation. Had we been savvier, and had we been more experienced – dare I say it, also a little older – we may have fought that decision, gone to another provider or charity, and started again. We could have gone to our landlord and asked for a three-year contract. It was, however, such a low blow that we didn't bother. We were so heart-broken that someone had told us we weren't allowed our dream because we were too successful for council housing and not successful enough to afford our own house, something my generation were increasingly priced out of anyway. The irony is that, once the 'system' catches up with 'generation rent', they will realise something will need to change and act on it. Only recently have laws been placed so that recently accepted adopters can apply for preferential social housing. That kind of availability would have been so very useful when we were applying – the frank and abrupt response from them was, quite honestly, one of the most damaging elements to our then application and the lack of enthusiasm to go through it again.

The luxury of family planning to this extent is something many young biological parents do not have. All this preparation for adding a new little one to our home, I think, could and should be made compulsory. There's always the 'accidental' pregnancy but family planning certainly wasn't in my Sex Ed class and I'm pretty sure it's not in the curriculum now. In September of this year, 2020, the Children and Social Work Act 2017 comes into law. In recent years, there have been regular calls to make SRE (Sex and Relationship Education) compulsory, often alongside Personal, Social, Health, and Economic Education (PSHE). This is also in addition to the updated guidance to reflect the changing pressures on young people, particularly important today with the dangers of sexting and online grooming. The content can still be determined by schools to a certain extent, but much of it is compulsory even in religion-focused schools, which is brilliant in my opinion. One particular relevant element to me is the law stating that schools, even primary, are free to determine how they address LGBT-specific content. This initially sounds disappointing. However, the Department of Education expects, 'all pupils to have been taught LGBT content at a timely point', and that 'they should ensure that this content is fully integrated into their programmes of study for this area of the curriculum rather than delivered as a stand-alone unit or lesson'. You'd be mistaken for thinking this was enacted years ago. It's not even in place as I write this. It will probably be closer to 2040 before they address the extended more widely used acronym of LGBTQ+.

Our first attempt proved to us a number of things. First of all that the social worker we first met, who looked a little frustrated having to deal with us, probably was. I can't blame that on anyone, but it wasn't us, it was him. We also now realise that they are so financially motivated that they don't waste their time on couples that 'might' not make it through selection or panel. They want a sure thing to fill their quota. As we are now seasoned foster carers, we understand the system so much better than we did back in 2010. It's not personal – its financial – and that's okay because now we know. We also learnt to listen to the dog more often; she's a better judge of character than either of us.

A year after making that first enquiry to adopt, we got married. It was a grand old affair on a budget. Our guests had no idea what to expect from a 'Gay Wedding', so we turned the volume up to the maximum. Cocktails galore, speeches, songs, music, and everyone had a pretty awesome time I'm sure. We even did the conga, because that's what you do. I had pulled a lot of strings. The boys from Jamie's were cooking, the staff from the pub were serving tables and doubled up as the most awesome guests. An old colleague of mine, now working at the Savoy, handled the cocktails. My best friend handled the wine, which was supplied at cost or donated by my supplier contacts, including the Rothschild winery. I caught up with friends I hadn't seen in years, it felt like it was yesterday. Those friends around me at our wedding showed me so much support, it was just what we needed. When I left school, I was still pretty angry with life in general. I took that out on a lot of my close friends, and I certainly regret that. Having to lie about yourself to everyone around you during the time when you are supposed to be creating bonds for life is really hard. Being gay specifically, and going through puberty, is a big time in any young man's life. Trying to tell boys I fancied them was impossible so I always ended in catastrophic failure. I fell in love with every good-looking guy I met. I wish I hadn't ruined those friendships so badly and would have handled them much better now. Some of them were at my wedding and understood completely, giving me a lot of closure during a testing time of my life. 2011 was a better year.

3

2013 – Second Attempt

2013 – We waited 18 months to hear anything back from TACT. We sent over a quick email:

Hi Jack,
It's been a while. We would love to catch up with you and update you on our situation. We're very confident that adoption is right for us now.

Not sure if he remembered us, eighteen months was not long enough for us to forget the emotions of the day we were told we couldn't adopt. Maybe we were so unsuitable after all. On the other hand, it was the same employee. We were glad he answered and didn't either ignore us or had moved on to another post. The reply:

Larry,
Can you give me a call on Tuesday as I am on duty.
Kind regards,
Jack

I promise you I'm not paraphrasing; this was the actual response. Tuesday came, and we called. Answer phone. We left an excited message. We never heard back from him. We were in a place where, for many years, we'd been talking about it, three years applying for it, and now we were just so deflated and down. We were so horribly disappointed with the whole process. I understand that, from his point of view, it was not a life-changing moment for him. One more message to get back to. However, for us, it was the most important email we could have ever sent. The most important voicemail we could have made. It was the difference of being the crazy old cat lady or a family.

We could have picked up the phone again, called again, and not cared if we sounded desperate. The reason we didn't was that we didn't want to admit we were desperate.

Desperation: A state of despair, typically one which results in rash or extreme behaviour.

We couldn't admit to ourselves that we had been rash or extreme. It sounds so finite, the end of something, and we hadn't even started. We are also not the kind of people to be defeated. We admitted to ourselves that perhaps it still wasn't the right time. There was some other life-force steering us on another path. Whatever craziness we would explain our current juncture with was all just smoke and mirrors. What we really wanted was to get on with the process and start a family of our own.

The maternal or paternal clock that exists in all humans must have been going off because it became part of daily conversations with friends and family. We would be at lunch, and it would come up every time. Our mothers, in particular, who are keen to hang on to their youth through the life of grandchildren, would be the most interested. Other family members, too, though, were concerned and excited in equal measures and would regularly ask how our application process was going. Not an easy conversation to have. Did we tell them about our apparent failure? We would resign to easy responses like 'we're not ready', 'we're having too much fun', 'we need to earn more money'. None of which was true as the desire, and paternal feeling was burning strong, we just couldn't get past the first hurdle it appeared.

4

2017 – Third Attempt

We were buying a house. We had been saving relentlessly for the past four years, taking advantage of the first-time buyers initiatives that the government had set up. Looking into every possible way onto the housing ladder. London was definitely out of the question. We could never afford two bedrooms inside Zone four, so we knew we had to move into the country somewhere. We were both country bumpkins anyway, so always knew that, if we were going to bring up children, it would be out of the city. We worked out that with our salaries, our ability to save, and the government initiatives, it would take nine years to save enough for a deposit. We had gotten used to that piece of information.

My father, who was a staunch businessman and an Essex boy at heart, was not the best father figure for me to aspire to be like. When he found out I was gay, he tried very hard to be understanding. He wouldn't discuss it with friends and hardly acknowledged it in public. With his tongue a little loosened by brandy, he would often tell me his honest feelings. It was hard to understand as he was my best friend growing up. I am still ribbed by my siblings for being the favourite. We were inseparable, until I came out. I promised this isn't going to be a coming out story, so I'll spare you the details. His parenting of me changed from best friend to distant parent. Offering me advice in riddles and referring to ancient poetry as a source of his newfound enthusiasm for the English language, which he was studying at Holloway University. I only recently realised how jealous I was of his new 'best friend', William, or Willy, as he called him. His new best friend was outrageously gay. The way he spoke and walked spoke volumes and he was younger than me by at least two years. My father had dumped his gay son, who was obviously a disappointment to him, and replaced him with an even gayer version. I had no way of understanding how that relationship started or why I was jealous of it. Perhaps the only reason I didn't come out sooner and be more gay than I did was because he would often publicly voice his homophobic opinions, which included bringing back hanging or shooting for the sin of homosexuality. That is, of course, unless you're a cute blond teenager called Willy, then you're allowed round for Sunday lunch with the family.

He passed away in November 2016 after a three-year battle with cancer. He was trying to marry his fourth wife, so I had very little emotional connection during his final years. I was best man at his second wedding, didn't bother turning up to his third, and this one I barely knew. He certainly wasn't lonely after he left my mother. My brother was there for him in his final moments, and my sister dutifully picked up all the pieces afterwards as the eldest. As awful as it is to lose a parent – I do so desperately wish he was still alive – I wish he was the dad I remember from when I was six as opposed to the dad I remember when I was sixteen. That dad was awesome. In his will, he left us a legacy and some cash, which boosted our own savings to a point where we could finally afford our dream country house. We fully intended to use my inheritance for the benefit of others. Any house we bought would be shared with everyone we know and love. We also knew that anyone in the future who cares to join us would also be loved. We won't leave any kin behind when we go, so I'm pretty sure we will leave a financial legacy behind us, too, for the benefit of others.

We started to consider starting a family again. We weren't going to make any mistakes this time round. We were certainly going to do our homework. I contacted as many people as I could; current carers, adopters, adoptees, and youth professionals. I was fortunate to be still involved with the Army Cadets, so I had a lot of contacts. We were a little unsure as to whether we wanted to adopt or now start considering foster care. None of our contacts could give us a steer either way, so we collected information on both.

Collins Dictionary terminology:
Adoption (verb) If you adopt someone else's child, you take it into your own family and make it legally your son or daughter.
Foster (verb) If you foster a child, you take it into your family for a period of time, without becoming its legal parent.

In summary, adopting would mean that, after a certain time, we would be totally responsible for that child's care as their legal parents. They would be 'ours' in every legal sense of the word. We could take them on holiday, cut their hair, dress them as we wanted – the works. Now that sounded like exactly what we wanted. Then there is the downsides. You may not get the court order of adoption; birth parents tend to fight before and after the adoption takes place. The child might come with emotional 'baggage', to name but a few of the many warnings we were given. Then there's the mental strain of the process, which we were only too experienced with already. Our research was thorough, but when it came to opinion, many were hesitant to give it. It felt like our friends, family, and contacts were mitigating blame for some reason. If our story ended in a nightmare, our many colleagues and associates would not be liable. It was a strange environment, not like buying a dog, everyone has an opinion on that. It also felt that, if things did go really wrong, there would be an element of 'I told you so' about it.

Regarding social acceptance and the press, we still had the *Daily Mail* story in the back of our minds. We also had recent public perception of London to deal with. The London Bridge terrorist attack had just happened, so the whole world felt a bit dangerous. World politics was completely off the sanity chart at that moment. Trump was in power, we were leaving the EU, and Far Right or Far Left were now common household terms. It was a reality as opposed to a history book. There were actual lunatics believing Donald Trump was a Divine leader and that Allah would save those who made the ultimate sacrifice with the additional reward of twenty virgins in the afterlife. The mind boggles at the thought.

It was such a minefield of opinion, literature, blogs, vlogs, and then our families had their say, too. My dearest mother, who I love more than life itself, was constantly asking me, 'Are you sure?' As if I'd turn around and say, 'Actually, I've changed my mind, dogs only from now on.' I know she is only doing her job of protecting me from emotional hurt. I also bully her now a little over it. Even though her intentions were genuine, it was only making me more confused. My mother shared the story about her adopted sister joining the family. How hard it was for her mother and father. My adopted auntie was mixed race, and the bullying was rife as a child. I can't imagine for a second how tough that was, how strong my grandmother was to cope with it. The '50s were a time of society slowly changing to be a little more cosmopolitan, but the country was still a little fresh from the war, and the Swinging Sixties hadn't quite kicked in yet. I couldn't even fathom the multitude of challenges faced by everyone involved. There wasn't even a happy ending. My auntie took her own life many years after leaving home. How am I supposed to digest that information? Was I forewarned and foretold? One thing is for certain, both heterosexual and homosexual parenting journeys are full of emotional tidal waves.

Fostering, on the other hand, was completely different advice. In my naivety, I was thinking it was all the same thing. Looking after other people's kids, right? Well, it comes with the same level of emotional craziness as my advice for adoption came with. Some of the advice we received was totally bonkers:

'You can't cut their hair without permission.'

'You're not allowed to hug them.'

'All of them are damaged.'

'None of them will love you like a real child will.'

'It's such thankless hard work.'

'Social workers are really hard work. None of them are any good.'

'The money is the best bit.'

There was one incredibly sound piece of advice that I got from a child in care. He was an army cadet and doing pretty well. He was attentive, respectful, and appeared emotionally together. I asked him if he minded me asking about his journey, which he didn't. I told him I was thinking of becoming a foster parent. Without hesitation, he told me to do it. He was clearly passionate about the need for more good foster carers in the world and that it was a truly wonderful calling in life. I asked him if he had any advice for me. His words were perfect, and I have lived by them in my capacity as a foster parent ever since, 'Don't do it just for the money, we always know.'

Yes, there is money involved. It's called professional parenting for a reason. What I have come to realise in this environment so far is that there are plenty of foster carers out there who do it as a career, and that's great. His advice was not to do it 'just' for the money – that was the matter of fact. Do it because you have a lot of love to give, do it because you are caring and genuinely want to help, do it because you want to. Like with everything in life when it comes to employment. If you enjoy your job, you never work a day in your life. Foster carers that treat their children as income, only seeing them as that, are missing the point. That was his advice.

You can see how this was rather confusing for us. It felt like everyone was trying to put us off and just enjoy being gay. My friends would look at my new Audi TT (Robin's treat) or Range Rover (company car) and tell us how lucky we are not to have kids. DINKs as they called us, Dual Income No Kids. This was used a lot to describe us. It was actually offensive and hurtful towards our feelings. Little did they know, we'd give up everything to have a family of our own. Maybe I'd keep the Range Rover. Friends would literally be congratulating us on not having kids, how lucky we were not to have the burden of social pressure to procreate. All we really wanted to do was steal their children and run away. Flashes of the child catcher from Chitty Chitty Bang Bang come to mind. This would obviously not be a way I would suggest to start a family. There are many legal implications in stealing children from their parents, even if the parents are supportive and encouraging. Although the struggles of becoming a legal parent are hard, kidnapping is, I would imagine, even harder.

It was a fabulous gentleman, who was a friend of a friend, that helped us make up our mind. He was most recently a senior manager of a prolific fostering and adoption charity, specifically for same sex couples. The charity in question was PACT (parents and children together). Nauseating memories of our experience with TACT came to mind. He was gay himself and the data that came out of PACT that twenty seven per cent of all of their adoptive and foster parents were LGBT was good enough odds for me. If anyone knew what to do, it would be him. He was also now involved in a government think-tank on the challenges and the issues around fostering and adoption in our country. Surely, he was the guy to direct us. We met for coffee and asked our usual questions. He in turn asked his about us, too. After some rather pricey cappuccinos, we surmised that he couldn't give us advice as he felt an obligation to be impartial. Moreover, should his advice be ill received or against the written advice he was curating for the government, it could be miss-quoted. So, we danced around, not answering each other's questions, which was actually the most helpful conversation we'd had to date. By just talking and not giving advice, we were allowed to form our own opinions and answer our own questions. It was actually rather refreshing to talk to someone so well educated on the subject and not have to deal with his opinion on it. We left that meeting with a strong sense of purpose and a personal, unofficial, recommendation to contact the office of his former employer with his endorsement. We were going to adopt.

5

2018 – Kinship Care

We bought a house – with a dream to refurbish it into this amazing family home that we could live in forever together, grow old, and have lots of children running around our feet. First things first, make the house safe and get rid of the damp. The house was inhabited by the same couple for thirty-five years and they had run out of energy to run such a dwelling – the past five years of its occupation had taken its toll on the old girl, and it showed. The house, not the incumbent, you understand. The owners had actually carved out a plot in the garden and had renovated the stables in order to fit their needs now in their advanced years. It's wonderful to know they were so emotionally attached to the house we were moving into that they couldn't actually leave, even when they had to. I've secretly got my eye on the stables to do exactly that when I'm fed up with climbing the rather windy staircase. Said staircase came with a five hundred year old country cottage surrounding it, and it was in dire need of modernisation. It doesn't help that, unfortunately, I am completely and utterly useless when it comes to home improvement. I can't hang a picture without it being wonky, a hole the size of a sledge hammer in the wall, and three bent nails to tell the story of every attempt. So, completely renovating a five-bedroom house was probably not the best idea.

One evening, while nursing my interior design failures with a small glass of Riesling, we got a phone call from my husband's sister. One of our nephews had got into trouble with the police and was hanging around the wrong people. He needed to get out of town. If we didn't take him, he would need to go into the care system. Fuelled by our new-found energy about our decision to adopt a young person, and lacking any common sense, we listened intently to a story about a child in need.

We've got one on our doorstep begging to come in, instant family. Being fifteen-years-old, he's a little older than how we had imagined our family to start – still, family is family. My husband jumped in the car and drove the five hours to Cheltenham and back to pick him up. I finished my glass of wine.

Of course, we took him in. I believe one of my superpowers is helping troubled teenagers stretch their ability and limits. For ten years, I had been working with the army cadets where young people aged thirteen to eighteen were challenged and inspired to achieve more through the values of the military. I had seen a huge spectrum of young people cross my path and benefit from my experience, teaching, and general mentorship. Robin was blood and had helped bring this young scamp up, from changing him, bathing, and everything else in-between. We had a big house, partially renovated, with room for plenty more souls. We wouldn't need an assessment, social workers visits, court authority, or any of the other million boxes to tick for him to live with us. It sounds like we're exactly the place he needs to be. Plus, I need someone to hold the ladder.

Richard arrived at one-thirty in the morning. It was summer, so quite pleasant, and I was outside in the garden still waiting for their return. He appeared high on drugs and a little shy. That was okay for now. I gave him a big hug and told him that he should treat this like his home and relax. One thing we couldn't ever tolerate, though, was drugs, and he had to stop now, cold turkey. He could never touch the stuff again while he was under our roof. He agreed, that was all behind him, and he would never do it again. One thing we couldn't risk was any kind of criminal activity under our roof whilst in application for adoption. That would ruin us after all we had been through; nine years of applications, disappointment, and continued dead ends. It would be foolish to even risk any of that, even if it was for family.

"So, you're safe with us and will always have a home here, but you need to keep your nose clean – and help with the house. Lots of help," I started my fatherly advice.

"Yes, Uncle. Got any cake?"

He suffered from diagnosed ADHD, and he wasn't happy being on Ritalin, telling us the drugs make him feel nauseous and unsteady. They obviously weren't working otherwise he would have been in so much more trouble with the police. So, with his insistence, we agreed to keep him off the meds and support him naturally with love, affection, and good, hard, elbow grease to keep him busy. It worked for the most part. Coming off the ADHD drugs and having a new living environment was tough for a teenager and we had a hard time convincing him the new sober version of himself was better. He was strong and tall, so when he got aggressive it was always a difficult time. I had to wrestle him to the floor and restrain him on a number of occasions to stop him from hurting himself or us. We always forgave him and always accepted his apologies. He did make one too many fist-shaped holes in our walls, however. Some of them I was quite happy to forgive, considering I was probably knocking down that wall anyway. Some, however, were not.

When he put his fist through a window, requiring my entire first aid kit to repair his peeling skin, it made us realise the trauma both he and us were going through. Plus, my newly-laid kitchen floor was now splattered with fresh blood. He wasn't in 'the system', so we were getting no support whatsoever. We also didn't have to report any incidences to the social service, which we knew we would have to, should we be officially looking after him. We also hadn't seen or heard from his social worker. I presume she was happy to be rid of him. What we initially thought was a welcome break from social services and child professionals was actually to his detriment. When he put his fist through a window, we had no support whatsoever, and clearly needed it. We didn't feel we needed a paramedic, so nothing was reported at all. Had this been a 'looked after' child, it would have involved late night calls to the out of hours office, social worker visits, CAMHS specialists, psychiatrists, the works. Later on that month, he said he wanted to kill himself and that all he wanted was social services to pick him up. No-one was there to answer him. We got nowhere. In fact, the out of hours county helpline for children went something like this:

Me: 'My nephew lives with us and is threatening to run away, he's fifteen.'
Social Services Out of Hours: 'What's his name?'
Me: 'Richard.'
OoH: 'We have no record of him?'
Me: 'Why would you, his last social worker just dumped him with us. What do you recommend we do?'
OoH: 'I can't actually recommend anything at the moment until you've spoken to his social worker as I could contradict what they say.'

Me: 'Are you joking? How about some parenting advice?'

OoH: 'Sorry, there's nothing I can do.'

This conversation went on for about thirty minutes before I, too, was at wits' end about what to do with my own life, let alone Richard. They were not willing to even give me some kind of parenting advice. It was about three in the morning, and I was dealing with a very angry, upset teenager who probably just wanted a joint more than anything. This was the first lesson for us of having to deal with the social service teams in a real-life scenario. It was our first experience of just how political the whole thing can be, how territorial, and how unhelpful it can be at times. Richard was fully aware of the system and knew how to play it, something we would also need to get used to. As naïve as I was, I was just going along with it. It was a sign also of how underfunded the whole system was. Here was a boy who was clearly in need of professional help, of which we were responsible. He was getting nothing from them, little from us, and the one person he really wanted it from, his mum, had run out of energy and patience with him.

He finally went to bed. We said good night, and in the morning, we faced a new day. Some days were better than others, some days were downright awful. Then there were the days that were just brilliant. I called an old friend of mine to help me with the roof, I can't do anything remotely constructive on a building site remember. He was a roofer, which helped, but more importantly, he was brought up in the care system. I gave Richard to him for ten days while he re-laid all the tiles on the roof. This gave both of them some quality time together to talk about Richard's challenges and how he feels. Richard is also one of those people that has to remain busy and is not shy of hard work.

His ADHD requires constant feeding and long days of manual labour are the perfect remedy for that. Up at seven a.m. and on the roof until five p.m. every day. He was up and down the ladders like a monkey at the zoo, he was really enjoying it. At the end of the task, he was offered a full-time paid job – alas, he's too young. It proved to everyone that, with purpose, he is more than capable of being a high achiever. His medication, which was suppressing his character and personality, I believe wasn't helping. The remedy of good, honest work seemed to be working much better. More to the point, he didn't have a registered doctor with us, neither did he have a renewable prescription for his medication. With the right level of attention and focus, it seemed to me that he functioned much better as a human without it than on it. Yes, he would be calmer on Ritalin, but he was also less humorous, less charismatic, and generally less fun to be around. Off Ritalin and focused on a project was the best way to pass the time. There is no correct or incorrect way to manage ADHD and far be it for me to go against a medical opinion or prescription. What we did was try something different. A different approach, a different level of supervision, and an entirely different environment.

I paid him five pounds an hour for all the work he did. He spent it as unwisely, as expected, but I didn't mind. He wasn't on drugs, which was the point.

We took him on holiday to my childhood destination. It was something I really wanted to do – share my childhood successes. At the end of the day, that's all we knew on how to be as parents, drawing on our own experiences. The things that went well in our own childhood are our only examples of how to be good parents. Drawing on those experiences was my plan to change his view of the world. That vision, plus what we read in books, conversations shared with our partners, and to watch what others do was all we had. The Greek Island of Paxos was a place that held such wonderful memories for me of incredible family holidays. It is also the place I went when I was eighteen and pretty angry. When I left school a little earlier than planned, I jumped on a plane to this island and stayed there for six months. The people on the island are so beautiful in their heart that it is a place you can't be angry. Life feels like it stands still, worries melt away, and you can breathe. I thought it may be just the cure he needed, somewhere to experience a life that doesn't involve drugs, knives, or gangs. We had an amazing time, filled with laughter. He got toothache, which didn't help. Such are the perils of parenthood. I had hoped that the holiday was going to be miracle cure, that he was going to come back a grateful and centred young person with a driving desire to achieve in life. Like I had twenty years before. No such luck, unfortunately. Between his toothache and dire need to irritate my husband, Robin, the standard holiday arguments were a stark reminder of what holidays with kids are like, teenage kids at that.

When we got home, we tried desperately hard to get him into a school. His social worker had finally given us parental authority, but he was still not in 'the system' so he got none of the benefits of being a looked-after child. Neither did we get any financial support, not that it was a concern or reason. It would have been nice, that's all. The schooling system didn't want to know. The council gave him two hours of tutoring in the local library. This was their way of fulfilling the government promise to ensure everyone has some form of education. Apparently two hours in a library constitutes an education. He would study maths, English, and science. He was naturally mathematic anyway without any formal education in the matter. He could work out mental arithmetic quicker than me. I like to think I'm quite good at maths, he was better. He was able to calculate seemingly impossible maths without hesitation; I'm not talking Rain Man level, but he was talented.

One day, I picked him up from his tutoring and, as always, quizzed him on his day and the content of his learning. He proudly presented a sock snowman puppet full of rice, he's fifteen remember. When I quizzed him on its validity to his education, he said it was because it was the last lesson before Christmas. It really did disappoint me with reference to the education system and how it was failing him over and over again. This led to him becoming bored, anxious, and desperately depressed with his life. He had his two enthusiastic gay uncles and a sixteen-year-old blind dog for company. Any sane teenager would naturally roll their eyes at the thought. He had left all his friends, girlfriend, and family on the other side of the country. We did manage to get him into the local rugby team, which he really enjoyed. The focus required to maintain team loyalty for eighty minutes really helped him. He made friends, found purpose, and genuinely was also very well behaved. He helped the team win the county cup and the process of working hard for something, getting rewarded and recognised, was a big help. We were trying everything we could to normalise his life with us. It was important to us that we presented him with every opportunity, and if something stuck, then we were doing a good job. It wasn't easy and he fought back a lot. His attachment issues with his mum and siblings were easy to identify but not easy to provide the right level of support for. He hankered to be home but knew it would never last.

What the local council didn't realise is that their insistence for him to be educated was actually making him worse not better. I had gotten Richard a job on a local farm in the summer for an ex-employer of mine. It was hard work, but it was honest work and he enjoyed it. His direct supervisor had a son with similar behaviour issues who was also working there, so she knew how to handle him and manage him brilliantly. We drove him the forty-five minute journey every morning and picked him up every afternoon. We bought him work clothes and ensured that he reported back each evening on how his day was going. He couldn't stay in that job because he had to go to school. A school that didn't exist. He couldn't go to college without English and Maths GCSEs either. So he wasn't allowed a job, couldn't get into school, and couldn't get into college. He wasn't allowed home to spend time with his brothers and sisters. Now, most of this is driven by his own life choices and he put himself in this position. Many would say, 'It's your own fault.' He, however, wasn't being given the opportunity to get himself out of this situation either. This would drive anyone to a feeling of complete failure. The system was letting him down time and time again.

The inevitable was bound to happen, despite all the warning signs and the desperate cries for help, Richard had had enough. He ran away one day because we had a falling out over bedtime. He was so angry with me, or himself, he thought he had no choice. I was also angry with him for not being more grateful, more determined to be successful, and more willing to engage with life. As his kinship guardians, we had no formal training. Like biological parents, we had no experience. We also didn't bring him up for the previous fifteen years of his life so didn't have that unconditional support that goes with time. He told me he was leaving, he would rather live on the streets than our house. I called his bluff and told him that was fine, lunch would be at one p.m. if he was hungry. I desperately wanted him to stay but, in the heat of the moment, you can say some silly things. I had our neighbour round at the time, who doubles as our electrician and sounding board for parenting as he has two sons. One of which also had a tough teenage period. Richard came back four times, asking for money, for food, where are his trainers, where's his phone. It proved to me that he didn't really want to run away. He just wanted me to react. I wasn't going to give in. My attitude to his tantrum was to ignore it. The last time he left, he slammed the door. He didn't return. It wasn't for another hour that I got a call from the police. At some point in the past six months I had given the NHS my number as an emergency contact, probably the dentist. I had no idea how they knew to call me. I'm only grateful they did rather than anyone else. I had a sense of responsibility for him. To worry his mother or my husband would have been, to me, a sense of failure. My heart was in my mouth, adrenaline kicks in, and everything slows down a bit.

Policeman: 'I'm looking for the legal guardian of Richard.'

Me: 'Yes?' [heart in mouth]

Policeman: 'You are down as a contact for next of kin.'

Me: 'Yes.' [stopped heart now in dry mouth]

Policeman: 'We have him. He was found on a bridge over the motorway threatening to jump.'

Me: 'Shit.'

Policeman: 'We haven't arrested him, but we need you to come down to the hospital and we may need to section him if we can't release him back into your care. A CAMHS specialist will need to assess him.'

Me: 'I'm on my way.'

We blamed ourselves for a bit, then blamed the system. He

blamed himself. There was lots of blaming. This was followed by lots of tears. He wouldn't talk to a mental health specialist, and wouldn't talk to the nurse or the pastor, who was hanging around A&E. It took three hours to see a representative from CAMHS and Richard wasn't impressed one bit about the situation. I guess he was embarrassed at the drama, embarrassed by the confusion and what strain he had put on everyone he loves.

Our first introduction to CAMHS was interesting. Another completely underfunded part of the NHS and care system. Two weeks after the incident, CAMHS finally set a meeting for a mental health specialist to assess Richard's mental wellbeing. They were brilliant with Richard, knew exactly what to say and how to say it. Obviously well-rehearsed in this type of thing and got straight through to him on his level. They admitted that they were completely under-staffed and that they would prefer to just sign him off as healthy and give him back than give him any kind of treatment. This blatant honesty was surprising for me, but I guess their reasoning was that it was a well-known fact that mental health in the NHS is under-staffed so why deny it now. They did, however, admit that he showed many of the signs of being autistic and he was most likely on the spectrum. The official diagnosis, however, had an eighteen-month waiting list at that moment, which has the possibility of increase. The best approach was to work it out for yourself and do what you think was best.

I have worked with plenty of autistic kids, usually high functioning. The army cadets can be great for children with Asperger syndrome, a form of autism that is relatively low on the spectrum. I had identified many of the symptoms and behaviours in Richard for a while now and had tried to respect his actions as a symptom of this. He got confused easily, couldn't listen to reason, and had trouble with sarcasm and ambiguity. You couldn't insinuate anything, it had to be a direct instruction. Many people would just think he's uneducated. However, he had some real issues with focusing and concentrating. He is diagnosed ADHD, but I believe that was a simple diagnosis. They didn't give him enough focus to work with him further. He was also on medication that 'calmed' him down. It made him docile and certainly did nothing for his focus. When he first arrived with us, he begged me not to make him take the medication. I'm quite a pushover when it comes to things like this and personally I don't agree with medicating ADHD. I believe this behaviour can be managed with positive energy and counselling. I was right, for most of the time. As I said before, it's not for me to disagree with a professional diagnosis or prescription, but what the ladies at CAMHS taught me was to adapt and work out what's best through experience. Would we have ever got to this stage, though, had he continued to take them? That may be true. His personality, however, his real personality, would never be able to shine whilst on medication. His real personality is loving, caring, and funny. If you let him be himself, he is the most polite and charming young man. Butter wouldn't melt and the ladies certainly enjoyed his presence.

So now our possibly autistic, angry, rapidly growing, teenage nephew with suicidal thoughts and actions was just released back into our untrained and unqualified hands. That was a real shock – still no answer from his previous social workers, but at least our local county had heard of him now. Still no education programme, no counselling diagnosed and in fact the opposite. If anything, the NHS acknowledged the problem and openly admitted that they have no facilities to help. It wasn't long before it kicked off again, and this time he broke his promise to us about the drugs. It had taken him nine months, but he found a local dealer who was willing to sell to him, although he swore blind he got it for free. I doubt that. I'm still trying to work out what he might have stolen and sold for the money. We did what we promised him we wouldn't, we gave up. It didn't feel as bad, considering he had broken his promise to us. We knew then that we were under qualified, under experienced, and lacked any form of formal training to take on such a child with special needs. We also realised that we desperately needed help from the local services if we were ever to make it work. This child needed specialist therapeutic counselling. He was sent back to his hometown and placed into care. The very system we tried to keep him out of was now his only hope. Costing the government now a hefty chunk of money that could have been used to support us instead. He was now in another household, who didn't and wouldn't love him as much as we did. It was, however, the best place for him. They managed to get him into a school, got him a psychiatrist, and got him all the support he needed. He was back on his meds for ADHD, and it all looked great in comparison to the mess we had gotten into not weeks before. He was helpful, kind, and popular.

This made us think again about our prospects as potential adoptive parents and would we want to continue. We certainly agreed that another fifteen-year-old with ADHD and possibly autism wasn't the ideal family we envisaged, but we also agreed that we handled it as best we could and a year out of our lives to help Richard get the leg up he so desperately needed was well worth it – we were pleased with our prospects and our abilities.

6

19 January 2019 – The Bullies Get Bullied

We went to visit Richard after a couple of weeks in his new home. We wanted to take him out for lunch to let him know we were still thinking of him daily and that we hadn't given up on him completely. We went go-karting with one of his brothers and popped into town for a burger and milkshake. Real quality time that was a far cry from where we had left him only weeks before. Frustrated and angry, back on drugs, and we were so disappointed in that. We had ended our relationship with a big bust up that involved the police and a night in the cells for Richard. We had hoped it would give him some sort of wake-up call. It hadn't. What appeared to be working was a more professional care system environment for him and we were so very pleased for that.

That evening, after dropping Richard at his foster carers home, we stopped by his mum's house. She insisted on taking us out for a drink to thank us for everything we had done for him. It was a small gesture that, although it's not normal nowadays for us to go out to bars in the evening, we obliged. That evening was set to change everything once again, forever.

I woke up in a prison cell feeling so terribly awful. I wasn't drunk. I had managed to control the urge to neck pints of warm pinot grigio for some reason. What had happened, though, would start a chain of events that would lead us along a completely different path. My husband had managed to get himself on the wrong side of the local security guard in a high street pub. We were from London, where we believe the security guards are of a slightly better level of experience and professionalism. We are also used to being openly gay, as opposed to years of having to oppress those physical displays of affection. It is the twenty-first century now, and we wrongly hoped a certain level of acceptance was normal across the country, not just in certain parts of London. In London, bouncers are not of the inclination that homosexuals are not welcome in 'straight' pubs. On this particular night at Yate's of Cheltenham, it seems to be a slightly different story. They took an instant dislike to us as an obvious gay couple in a predominantly straight environment. Before I realised what was happening, my husband was being dragged out of the venue by two guards. Obviously, I took an instant disliking to this and told them to leave him be. I am a qualified door security guard myself and a licensee. I have worked the door of some of London's biggest nightclubs. My years on the door of a gay nightclub in Cheltenham whilst at university will prepare you for anything. If you've ever tried to break up an alcohol-fuelled girl only fight in Gloucester, you'll know what I mean.

After a few choice words about 'us fags' in 'their bar', I stood my ground. Being trained in approved restraint techniques and with several years of martial arts training, it wasn't difficult for me to remove their grip on my husband. I stood between them and said something along of the lines of them having to get through me before they lay a hand on my husband again. When the police turned up, the security guard in question needed to go to hospital. He pressed charges and, because he needed hospitalisation, it was an automatic arrest for me. In the cold light of day, once a full investigation had taken place, I was cautioned for battery. Although there was no physical evidence, they thought the person had a strong enough case for a conviction and he wasn't giving up. He wanted to take it to court. I got on very well with the custody sergeant, who explained to me that he had no choice but to charge me with something. I refused legal representation on the grounds of my innocence and agreed to the caution solely in order to get to a bed that was not made of concrete. A hasty decision I will live to regret.

My military record as a cadet instructor and obvious good conduct in the local community did give me a good standing to defend myself. However, I also refused a lawyer as I really didn't think it was necessary. The advice from the custody sergeant was that, due to my pleasant nature whilst being arrested, calmness under pressure, community standing, and being a general nice guy, he had the ability to reduce the assault charge to the caution. This was the lowest he could go. This would mean that there would be no conviction and I would not need to disclose unspent convictions between now and a court date. After I explained the details of the adoption application process, we spent most of the investigation time talking about that. He said he had no choice, but a caution was the safest way to go. With no previous record, I should be fine to convince any agency of my good nature, as I had done that day. I took the caution.

I called my Army Commandant that afternoon to tell him I had just got a criminal record, his response in my defence was emotional. He was a London barrister at the High Court. He told me I was an idiot for not getting representation, I know that now. However, he backed me one hundred per cent in my actions as he knew the person I actually was. He knew of my nature and of my temperament. He had seen me work with young people for years and get the best out of them. He had seen me face homophobic bullying with patience and tact. He knew me as the person I really am, not the person the police, security guards, and that high street pub group had misinterpreted me to be.

I called the adoption agency next. They were a little less understanding. Their responses was on the safe side of cautious. They didn't know who I was, had no history of me, so therefore no sense of loyalty to defend me or support me. They dropped us like a stone. We pleaded for a response and a face to face. We told them to come to our house and meet us properly. Have a cup of tea and find out who we really are. They agreed to a meeting at their head office once they had spoken to their superiors. I feel that perhaps their agreement to a meeting was for one reason only, to shut us up. I believe strongly, however, that had any of them come to our house, seen what normal and calm people we really are, we would have had a better chance to defend ourselves.

The meeting came and we dressed to the nines. Robin and I dutifully and respectful entered the offices. We were basically begging for the life we had come to expect would just happen. A police caution based on no evidence was potentially going to cast a life sentence of being DINKs. We had a brief time to explain the situation to them. At the end of our conversation, they just informed us that the agency had made the decision not to progress our application. They felt my actions did not reflect their values and standards in child care. They could not trust me not to be aggressive or violent towards a child. They did not feel safe in the knowledge of this information and in letting us adopt a child. On reflection, I would have preferred to have this decision told to me over the phone now and not put all the effort in to come and see them at their office. Why drag me up here if you have already made up your mind. It is not a legal requirement to stop people from adopting who have cautions against their names. The law states that a person may not adopt a child if they have been convicted (a caution is not a conviction) of a crime against a child. Therefore it was their discretion whether or not to progress our application. Their discretion that they did not spend very much time deliberating on and did no research whatsoever on the evidence. Once again, we find ourselves at the mercy of an agency that appears to value the rate of successful placements over the people they are placing with. A guaranteed placement is more profitable than a failed one. I pity anyone who has aspirations of adoptive parenthood who has a colourful past. The most disappointing thing for me was that they had already decided what the outcome was before we even set foot in the room. Predetermined decisions based on unsubstantiated claims of unsuitability – a theme of our application process so far.

Now, having already faced rejection for adoption because we were too young and didn't own a house, I figured I was used to it by now. I did have a problem with the two twenty-year-old graduates acting on behalf of this adoption charity. They obviously had nothing better to do with their time than waste mine, informing me of a decision that was clearly already made. The supervisor didn't bother getting up from her desk to talk to me personally. It was the fact that they judged me on the ability to be a good father to a child based on an incident that was actually rather honourable. How dare they judge me, criticise me, and pass me over on my dream. With this in mind, I decided to tell them just that. I was a little tired of failing because of bureaucracy, policy, and process. Tired of agencies focusing on the results and the money. I'm doing this for the love of being a parent in any capacity. I care not for your achievement figures.

I'm pretty sure they must have left that meeting saying to themselves how lucky they were to have made that decision because I was quite emotional and showed it. My eyes welled up and my husband had to put a hand on my shoulder to calm me before I said something I may have really regretted. In my mind, I had defended the honour of my husband as he was being bullied by five homophobic security guards. I do not lack confidence when faced with bullies. Some of my previous training is muscle memory and a number of defence techniques that include incapacitating people. The gentlemen in question were lucky, in my mind, that I restrained myself as I did. I knew then that my actions could put our adoption application in jeopardy, so I was very careful. All my restrained, careful, and controlled actions counted for nothing in the eyes of these social workers. They had made their decision and it was final.

I was so desperately upset. My actions had created a chain of reactions that resulted in us never being able to start a family. I am still emotional about it now. One little situation that I believe I was innocent in changed our lives forever. What if I just fought it in court? I rang the police station and asked if I could rescind my admission to the caution. They let me know I had signed the document and I couldn't now go back on it. So, I called the Police Complaints Commission. I told them I wasn't made aware of the consequences of my actions. I told them the whole story and they were sympathetic to my cause. The case was picked up by an inspector in Gloucestershire, who called me and was also sympathetic. The custody sergeant who had advised me on the caution in the first place called me. Although I had raised a complaint about him, he too was sympathetic. Again, the advice stuck – the caution could not be reversed.

"What if I call the security guard personally and apologise?" I asked.

I had exhausted every possible idea. So, I resorted to apologising to the guy who homophobically attacked my husband with the support of his neanderthal mates. They had publicly humiliated and taunted me into a situation where I had no choice but to defend myself and my husband from continued abuse. It's not like us to permit people to continue to single out gay couples as an easy target. For decades, we have been marginalised as a group of society that deserves less. All around the world, that fight still goes on with incredible violence and bigotry. Young men are stoned, set light to, and thrown from tall buildings, all in the name of religion to 'protect' their purity against the devil's work. Such ignorance to love less, so I will not let it still be a part of society today and will defend it whenever I need to. I sometimes imagine, what if I just let us get assaulted. Perhaps I should have just walked away, but that's not my way. I stand up to bullies. Stonewall and Gay Pride fought hard for our right not to hide in the shadows. The law against homophobia changed in 2010 to make it illegal to incite hatred through homophobia, but it is rarely enacted and many police officers shy away from it. It was never an option when in custody. I'm pretty sure that if I was female and accused my attacker of abuse, the situation would have been very different.

I found it almost funny that I hold a commission from the Queen to 'act on her behalf in the leadership of men should she call upon my services'. This commission is evidence of the system's faith in me to have integrity. Something that perhaps did assist in showing favour towards me post-arrest, but what upset me more was the punishment I was receiving would last a lifetime. I don't blame anyone for what actions they had to take, I hold myself totally responsible. It is, however, the consequences of the collective that baffles me still now. Why deny a child in need a warm, loving home because of one incident that is marred with lack of evidence and a strong sense of honour at its core?

Denying us a family at the same time, destined for the life of being an old miserable gay queen harking on about the good old days. What are we going to do with a five-bedroom country home now? Selfish, I know, but there is only so many dinner parties I can hold.

7

20 January 2019 – What About Fostering?

I was complacent and I blamed myself. I even considered divorce as an option so my future ex-husband could adopt as a single parent. It didn't feel right. Of course, he was also steadfast in my defence as he was there at the incident in Cheltenham. It was in his honour I acted like I did. It was only because he was my husband that I jumped to his defence so enthusiastically. As I think anyone would, gay or straight. If a nightclub 'bouncer' was to aggressively drag another human along the floor, you would expect that person's significant other to jump to their defence.

I started to research the legality of suing, not sure what for. Not that it would do any good, perhaps it would make me feel better. I then started to look around for more agencies – surely not all are as shallow as the last one. I was wrong, every single agency wouldn't touch us. I got rejection after rejection after rejection. Some were even nice enough to write to me afterwards just to confirm the rejection. I was also advised to come back in ten years. Perhaps I could try in five, just to make sure.

It was at this point, faced with the constant rejection to adopt, that we discussed fostering as an option. We had just given up on Richard because we lacked the training and support to deal with him. There must be plenty of Richards out there who could use our help. We may also be able to get Richard back if we were trained to do it. How different it would be if we had the right support network and the right funding behind us to make it work properly. We did an all right job with him with no support. 'Professional parents' was a term we had not heard before, but maybe, just maybe, we could foster rather than adopt. We had discussed it before but dismissed it as what we really wanted was our own child. Don't forget, we had been 'advised' by others that fostering was thankless hard work and you weren't allowed to cut their hair without permission, etc. We had been given nightmare stories, including about one child who burnt down their foster carer's home. The situation we were in gave us little hope. Richard had given us the inspiration to foster, so why not.

I'm used to telling the homophobic bouncer story. I'd had to do it thirty times already, only to be denied an interview by every adoption agency in the country. I was so used to it that, I would just start the conversation with it.

The agency recruiter would call 'Is that Larry, I have your details here as you expressed an interest in becoming a foster parent.' Every call started the same, 'Yes that's me, I also have a police caution for battery, just FYI' would be my response. I would try it in different ways, but most of the time I was just direct. The response was always the same, 'Come back in ten years, try in five maybe.' Not one person wanted to meet me, not once did I get a sympathetic response. I was judged every single time and, more often than not, I would be so emotional after each call I was certain it would break me.

I continued to keep myself busy with refurbishing our five hundred year old country farmers' cottage. By early 2019, I had finished the house refurb and had been working for myself as a hospitality consultant for about a year. I started to believe I wasn't even very good at that either. Not a great business consultant and coach with such a disappointing outlook on life. My emotional and psychological state was getting a battering and we also knew that to be successful carers, we needed to be mentally strong to manage the challenges associated with looking after young people in the care system. It was a catch twenty-two situation where the emotional roller coaster of applying to be a carer was actually detrimental to our mental strength in being able to cope with being a carer.

I had to just pick myself up off the floor every time and say to myself, 'Don't give up, you prat.' Not quite sure I needed to be that tough on myself, but I was on the verge of breaking down. I felt like my house needed to be filled with people, otherwise what was the point. My own family were being purposefully distant at the time due to an internal family feud, so it really was a bit of doom and gloom. Might as well sell up, move back to London, and get a job. We had spent the best part of ten years preparing ourselves for country living with a family. 'Come on man, pick yourself up!' Robin would be metaphorically slapping me round the face.

One last go, I'm not being dramatic. It was literally my last hope. One last google of fostering agencies in the area. Foster Care Kent, or FCK as their acronymic, seemed appropriate as its similar dictionary cognate was a word I would repeat to myself regularly whilst banging my head on the desk.

FCK are an independent fostering agency with a very clear vision:

- Providing safe, secure, and nurturing foster placements where any child or young person can thrive emotionally.
- Supporting foster parents with fostering training, support, and professional development.

• Listening to children, young people, foster parents, staff, and local authorities to ensure quality services.

They are specialists in therapeutic fostering, an approach to fostering where the carers have been part of the therapy process for the child. In addition to a number of other approaches, including parent and child, emergency, and even remand. As a therapeutic carer, we would receive additional training and be considered for more challenging placements in the future. Fine by me!

Emma, the recruiter for our Foster Care agency, called me back, 'Is that Larry? I have your details here as you expressed an interest in becoming a foster parent.'

They do all start the same.

My response was, 'Yes, that's me. I also have a police caution for battery, just FYI.' Emma seemed not to hear me as she proceeded, 'Yes, I'd like to book you in for a face-to-face at your place to catch up properly and go through a few questions.' I repeated myself, but again she insisted on coming to see us both. I couldn't believe my luck. It was just stage one. I had done two stage ones before so I knew exactly what I was getting myself into and it was not very exciting. I was, however, excited, perhaps too much. I know that if I could just convince one person that I was not this aggressive, violent bouncer-hater portrayed in my record, then we at least had a chance. That is the one thing I had been praying for, the chance to meet someone face-to-face in our house to show them how we were as a couple and how much love and care we can give a child in need.

Our meeting went really well. The police caution was obviously a topic that needed to be discussed, but we were really welcomed by Emma and the whole process put us at ease. Their relatively modern approach to the care of their children really suited our lifestyle and approach to parenting ourselves. We discussed the therapeutic element of caring and it seemed to resonate with both myself and Robin. We didn't know it at the time, but our parenting style was the same one they advocate. We were to be given all the training we needed and all the support we needed. Our experience with dealing with Richard was just what we needed to be prepared, but it also showed us how our lack of support was holding us back. The agency application gave us some assurance that we weren't a failure, as we thought. More like we had the experience necessary to prepare ourselves more for what challenges may lie ahead. Being a kinship carer for Richard and having to hand him over to another professional family was hard, and the empathy we now feel will set us up for the future when it happens again. It also increases our resilience to emotions, being able to deal with these challenging situations.

The next stage was for Emma to give feedback to her boss about us, including the dreaded black cloud that hung over me. Her boss was to make the final decision. That's all we really wanted. We wanted to be considered at least. If the answer was a 'No', that would have been fine with us because we would have done everything in our power possible. We hoped that the decision maker was of sound mind to see past the barriers and see us for who we were. Caring, loving, and capable adult role models with genuine reasons to foster children in need. The needier the better, in our mind, as we knew that our pleasure would come from helping those that needed it most. This agency seemed to be able to provide that as their services included full care for children who otherwise wouldn't be able to be placed in traditional foster homes. We would be that solution. We felt that we could offer an environment like no other; young(ish) gay couple with bags of energy, a wide variety of interest and hobbies, and with a beautiful home. Our slightly mad and very large extended family would welcome anyone into it with open arms for sure. It wouldn't matter how challenging the young person would be, whether they were disabled or had learning difficulties, we would make sure we were the very best pro parents any looked-after child could hope for.

To be a Foster Carer, you need at the very least a certain level of criteria to be filled before the application process continues and this was checked at the initial meeting – put simply these two things are:

One. We had available rooms in a secure home that we owned.

Two. We had the time and personal qualities to be a professional parent and carer.

Personally, we also had lots of questions about what to expect. We also had to squash the preconceptions we had heard of what kind of children we would get. We had to come up with a lot of answers, too. Emma put us at ease and treated us with respect. We drank tea, ate too many biscuits, and got on really well. I'm sure people like Emma get on with everyone, but her gregarious and kind nature really put us at ease. We learnt plenty too. Over time, fostering had changed over the past few years. Especially since the days of Workhouses in the nineteenth century, obviously. Then the 1926 orphanage and fostering act was passed. More recently, though, we were pleased to understand that the approach to gay couples had somewhat lost its front-page scandal and it was far more common. Although we would be their first in the agency and the only ones down here in Kent. No longer was it appropriate to treat children in care as different. In fact, it was actively frowned upon. The emphasis is on ensuring they have the same opportunities afforded to them as 'normal' children. Children living in the care of their biological parents had certain assurances in life than those who didn't. It was okay to talk about it, and it was okay to show love, have cuddles, and most importantly have fun. There is criteria about savings, spending on clothes, and meal plans. Children in care can't look like they're in care. Hollywood paints a usual stereotype, with the likes of Oliver Twist and Annie. Kids in the care system are dramatised into perceptions of what it would be like. The job of a foster carer is to protect them from that and ensure they feel like they have the very best support, akin to that of a 'normal' family. This journey was possibly the road we were supposed to travel on from the beginning. I'm not too sure which religion I believe in, if at all. I do believe in a higher power that we don't quite understand yet, and that our journeys are somehow mapped for us. Whether it's true or not, it's nice to believe in something. It's nice to believe that someone has a plan for us, and that it includes helping others in need. Our destiny, if you will, was not to have children of our own, neither was it to adopt. Our plan was to foster, to help others, and to give opportunities to young people that, without us, may never have been afforded to them.

8

February and March 2019 – The Form F

Once we had been officially accepted into the training programme, we had an assessment to complete first. The application process starts with being appointed an independent social worker. This person's job is to take you through the process of completing a Form 'F'. A Form 'F' is your application form to be a Foster Parent. It takes around three months to complete, and it's very detailed. Our independent social worker appointed to complete it was as approachable as Emma, with such a warmth about her it wasn't an interview or an interrogation. It felt like a chat with a matron at school. She was slightly older than us, had gold spectacles, and wore the most beautiful flowing dresses. 'Mrs Doubtfire' came to mind when we saw her, not because she resembled the most amazing Robin Williams I assure you. It was more because she personified that warm caring nature that he channelled for that particular movie.

Our appointed independent social worker's name was Lyndsey – she had such a passion for her job and she naturally put you at ease. Her soft tones in her voice could calm the most awkward of situations. Incredibly experienced and had a 'seen it all, done it all' approach, making you feel relaxed about telling her anything. I guess this is a desirable trait in order to encourage you to let any barriers down that you may have and open up. Honesty is very much the best policy here. Her job is to assess us as potential foster carers and, at the same time, provide us with the support to get through the application process. No point in lying about how we feel about certain minority children and then being matched with that minority child. She is obviously measured on the success of her applicants so she won't progress us without a level of certainty. This again put us at ease. The confidence she had with us was infectious and we in turn were confident that this time we might actually get through it. Coming from a position of doubt for such a long time, it was a relief to be made to feel like this could actually happen.

The family tree exercise was interesting. I have a relatively normal family tree – two siblings, a mother, and father deceased. Two offspring from my sisters' side and grandparents all deceased. Apart from cousins and international uncles and aunts I had seen twice in my typical life time, my family tree was relatively easy compared to my husband's.

Robin required his own meeting for a family tree. One of six from his mum's side, with a few half brothers and sisters elsewhere from his father's side. More than one stepfather and an estranged biological father. Of the five siblings from his mother's side, one is also gay. The other four between them have sixteen children. There is approximately ten other people involved in creating these sixteen children. As you can see, it's a difficult family tree to get on one piece of paper. Yes, they argue, we all argue, but they have a strength in numbers that outweighs anything I've experienced before. At least eight of the working age members of Robin's close family tree are carers in some form or another, so it definitely runs in the family. They are fiercely loyal and supportive of each other. Yes, they are a bit bonkers, but aren't we all. Apart from the Richard incident, which I put down to his ADHD, and a few nephews that were serving time, or had already, it was not a concern for me that Robin needed his own meeting.

Robin had to explain it in full to a third party in one afternoon and it was challenging to say the least. Eventually, I think we agreed to drop out any half siblings or distant blood relatives and just get to the people we know – their names, not nicknames. I have known most of his family for twenty years, many of the nieces and nephews I have known since babies. I have also understood that the entire family share a one common trait with each other. That same trait, too, serves them and their chosen careers so well. Each inherited a common chromosome that gave them a huge loving heart for each other, and it's obvious to see in each of them. It's the reason I fell in love with my husband so deeply and it's the reason I loved his entire extended family. This is why I also know that they will support our application to be foster carers with such enthusiasm.

In essence, it's his side of the family tree exercise that actually gives us the better examples to draw on for our experience to care for others. Between us, we have baby sat one or more of those sixteen nephews and nieces on several occasions, including entire weeks of school holidays, and the respite care for my sister-in-law. It's his side of the family we draw a number of examples of responsibility for a young person's life in our home. My side, in comparison, being average middle class, is also rather boring. My husband also has a lifetime of experience in a big family, which is what we were applying for. We had four spare rooms so, in essence, we were prepared to have them all filled with children in care. Those early conversations also answered that question for us. Being relatively inexperienced carers, it was doubtful they would approve three children, let alone four. We would only ever be approved for four if they were a sibling group, otherwise three is the maximum. We also had a vision that we would never give up on kids. I'm an emotional wreck when it comes to attachment anyway, so the idea of doing respite or short-term fostering filled me with dread. I obviously didn't tell Lyndsey this, I was a fine example of resilience. Perhaps she saw through my emotions anyway, knowing full well I would have trouble giving up a child to another family or back to their original family. With that in mind, it was recommended that our first placement would be a permanent placement, or so we thought. So if it wasn't a sibling group of four now, it never would be until that child aged out. Now, if that's a four-year-old, we're now talking fourteen years before we could fill all four rooms.

Next we talked about a timeline of events. Significant events, like death, marriages, and when we met. Also, where we lived and jobs. This is easier said than done. Often for millennials and the following generation, establishing themselves on the housing ladder is a thing beyond many means. Therefore, rented accommodation is the order of the day. In turn, landlords are keen to move out tenants every two years to benefit from price increases beyond the retail price index. This meant that, in the past ten years, we had moved five times. Before that, we were in a foreign country. Before that, we moved a further four times. Needless to say, we had to use the back of the form. My industry, too, is a rather transient one. Hospitality tends to favour young blood regularly to keep them modern and in touch. That has its benefits and negatives but again, for the untrained eye, it appears like job hopping. My partner, too, had changed careers and jobs with as much regularity as the amount of house moves. Writing it all down was also a calming process of reflection and gave us both the opportunity to go back through our histories. It included where we had lived as children, from birth to now. It was interesting and we still managed to learn things about each other we didn't know before. They do say, at the start of the process of Form F, is not to treat this as therapy, but it was hard not to. The very process of reliving the past twenty years was cathartic in itself and if we gained some therapeutic benefits from it, why not.

Lyndsey was as calm as they came, always friendly, warm, and welcoming. As I said before, she put us at ease. She had such a wonderful approach and let us lead the conversations. Sometimes they would go dramatically off track, losing the original question. It was her way of getting more honest feedback out of us and to watch us interact with each other. When I entertain at home, I'm happiest loading the dishwasher than I am entertaining guests. This was clear from our initial meetings, and it reflected in her account of us when the report was finally published. We are a balance of emotional and personality traits that together make us ideal to manage challenges and difficult situations. Little did we know, and we were warned to the point, that we would need to draw on these personality traits hard in order to manage the challenges that lay ahead.

We moved on to significant events and whilst my father had passed away relatively recently, within two years, he had been estranged from me for a while. Our relationship broke down shortly after coming out to him. Although he was accepting, he had plenty of underlying issues and, within four years of coming out to him, our relationship had broken down completely. Robin's biological and step fathers had passed within the past eight years too. We hadn't had much in terms of significant events aside from that. Apart from all the drama associated with

Richard and our own ability to generate a wake of emotional chaos, we were relatively boring in terms of the Form F. Perhaps that was a good thing, you don't find out till the end.

Next on the agenda would be the local area and the house. Where the school's area, social groups, and who of our circle of friends were in the local area. We are lucky enough to live next door to the local councillor and we have a great relationship with all our neighbours. All these things add up to a positive reflection on us and the environment that we are inviting these young people to share with us. We had spent a small fortune on renovating our five hundred year old farmers' cottage, so we were lucky in its presentation. Being a hotelier for most of my career, you can imagine the quirks we managed to afford ourselves. The original 1950s aga may present issues with crawling babies, so this was one of our challenges. This was followed by a flurry of health and safety additions for the next visit two weeks later. There were child-safe locks on everything, from the toilet seat to the garden well and everything in-between. We had possibly underestimated just how much danger is present when you don't consider it. The fire alarms, carbon alarms, security cameras, baby gates, cupboard locks, and toilet door locks you can open from both sides – it's just endless. It felt like we had to approach our house from a completely different perspective and start again. It wasn't that dramatic, but when we finished two weeks later, we were all very happy with the way the house was presented. You also need a desk, wardrobe, and bed in each room suitable for a child. We hadn't quite got the suitable for a child bit right and were encouraged to make it a little more child friendly. An incredibly fun trip to town, buying sparkly unicorn book-ends and life-sized stuffed animals, was possibly the highlight of the Form F. However, two gay men without kids shopping for attractive child-friendly quirks for their five-bedroom house did put us a little on edge.

References is a biggie in terms of the shared emotional trauma it can cause a close-knit group of supportive friends and family. It forms such a big part of Form F and certainly sparked a few debates. Unusually, we had already asked several people to provide references for the adoption application one year before. We had the unusual ability to look back with hindsight on whether we had chosen the right people, or had some people not been chosen, and this made us acutely aware of that. This caused a little difference in opinion on our part as most, if not all, of our friends are dual referees. We had been together for seventeen years, so everyone knows us both very well. Whose reference would be for who? It has to be both our mothers – we couldn't possibly ask one and not the other.

My ex-girlfriend has known me more intimately than most and acts as both a significant ex and as a referee. I am godfather to one of her children, so I know her appraisal will be favourable and perhaps not include the details of the day I ended our relationship, which wasn't pleasant. When we have confirmed our choices, we are not shown the reference result, probably something to do with GDPR. Some of our friends did indeed send them on to us separately and it was so lovely to read what our friends thought of us. Obviously, in this world, we don't tell people enough how much we respect, admire, or love them. Especially not when we're being told that the lives of young people are in the balance, so you better make it really good.

I also got my commanding officer in the Army Cadet Force to write an additional reference specifically around the police caution I had received. Again, it was incredibly favourable. If friends are rare in expressing their love in writing to you, it's even more unusual for a colonel of the army to do so. It was nice to read how much my efforts with the Cadet Force were appreciated and how my nature was never in question for the past ten years. Even relatively new friends of only eight years were extremely respectful in their assessment of us, which we are blessed to be in reception of. I have no idea why, but I was still pretty nervous. We were warned that panel don't often appreciate sarcasm, jokes, or innuendo. I had to warn my own mother not to tell stories about my involuntary addiction to removing all my clothes as a toddler and parading naked around the house. The panel did not need to hear that. Would my best friend from school tell them the story of hanging him up in the locker room by his shirt collar? I hope not.

Nerves play a big part of completing the application form, I guess it was natural to feel nervous. Finally, we were being considered as parents and it had been such a long road. I hope we don't mess it up this time. Then there is the feeling that you don't want to feel nervous in case the social worker picks up on that and thinks there is something more sinister. That thought in turn incites more nerves. Just when you think it's all good, they tell you about the social media checks and IP address search history checks. My anxiety at this point was through the roof. I knew my recent search history kept coming up with pictures of teenage boys' bedrooms. It surprises me still as it comes up in my emails at least once a month. It shouldn't have worried me, of course, as I was decorating Richard's room not long ago and wanted some inspiration. As a gay man, having his internet search history checked with teenage boys' bedrooms at the top of the list is going to make you sweat a little, no matter how innocent. Then there was that topless picture of Zac Efron that I had liked on Instagram, what would they think of that!

I have no idea what was going through Lyndsey's mind. Did she find our worries funny? Had she heard it all before? Been there, got the t-shirt mentality. I'm sure she has seen and heard a lot in her career, but for us it was personal. It felt a little intrusive but also liberating at the same time. Completely different from the two recently qualified teenage social workers at our adoption agency who couldn't have been more opposite in their demeanour. Her ability to get us to open up and relax was magical. We would even talk about why and when we argue with each other. Which we found out is probably some of the most stupid reasons to argue. Who unloaded the dishwasher? Who is going to walk the dog? Why is the window left open? The most famous of arguments, what temperature should the heating be set at? Or maybe they are the best reasons. We would never argue over money or politics or religion. The three biggies. This takes me back to the instruction of not treating the process as a therapy session, well – we couldn't help it. Lyndsey was too good.

When the report is published, you realise just how much you've been babbling on about the past, the future, and the present with your ISW. The printed version is heavy, and you have to read it to ensure that you agree with its content. It's all a true reflection of your conversations and you have to say you're happy for it to be submitted. This process of checking your ISW's work is the same as getting to do it all over again. There is also new bits you were not privy to at the time. Considering that some of the interviews between yourself and the ISW are done independently of each other, there is bit you did not take part in. This gave Robin great entertainment as he got to read about my formative years travelling in Europe, which until now I had not expanded on in too much detail. Lyndsey's interrogation techniques had opened me up like a book. I have no idea why I discussed those things with Lyndsey either, probably due to her superpowers of information extraction. I swear, if MI5 don't snap her up soon, they would have missed a trick. The Form F is over twenty thousand words of analysis and reflection on all the interviews we had together. The detail is surprising in every element of our lives. Who are our mentors in life and why? Who do we respect and look up to? Who are the people that have positively influenced our life? It's remarkable to have the opportunity to reflect on the influences that make you who you are. I could probably publish our form F as another book in itself. I'm pretty sure, however, it's only really interesting to us and the panel of experts judging us.

Some of the more interesting elements of the reflective report were how it was made relevant to our application to foster. Moving to Spain gave us experience of moving to a foreign country, relevant to fostering an asylum seeker. Robin had grommets as a child and consequently had to learn sign language, another benefit to the application. My private school was attended by a wide variety of different ethnicities, giving me experience of different cultures. It was interesting how every experience in my life can be used as a form of preparation in the life of a foster carer. It gave us confidence still in our lessons from the 'school of life' to make us the most suitable of professional parents.

During this time, there was also quite a bit of formal training required. Safeguarding is an obvious one, although I have done a number of these types of sessions with the Army Cadets. Pre-selection training and skills to foster are two pre-requisites that enable us to ask further questions and understand more of what it's like to be a foster carer. This is also the time where a number of potential carers can drop out of the process. Some of the realities of becoming a professional parent do put a stop to some people who perhaps thought they were ready, who actually weren't.

In the end of the dossier, you are given a recommendation. Ours was:

"I recommend that Robin and Larry are registered for two children, either gender, aged zero to eighteen. I recommend that they are registered for short term, long term, and respite placements.

Matching considerations:

I recommend that while Robin and Larry are gaining experience, they are not matched with complex placements and that while Richard (the applicants' nephew) remains as a regular visitor, that matching considers his needs."

Now all we had to do was pass panel.

9

24 April 2019 – Panel

It sounds scary, the word panel. I may suggest that they change it to 'socially exciting decision-making meeting'. Especially considering I had the overhanging topic that could prove tricky and it being our first one. A panel of professionals, experts in their chosen field. Every one of them had already read our Form F. That means everyone knew I left my girlfriend for another guy, even though he wasn't gay, and I wasn't out. Everyone knew Robin and I got together when he was seventeen and I was twenty-one. We had shared our entire life with Lyndsey, who we felt completely and utterly at ease with. Then these other eight people had read the entire twenty thousand word document. These strangers to our lives knew more about us than our own mothers. The adrenaline was pumping, and we obviously were thinking the worst, what if we don't get approved?

The panel consisted of several people we knew, knew of, or didn't know at all. Some were senior members of the charity that we had met or talked to a couple of times in the past. Some members were completely new to us and had backgrounds in psychology, child mental health, or schooling. There was also a seasoned foster carer who was a former policeman. Guess who's going to ask me about my police caution? We had received a document ahead of time giving us a little background on everyone, so it kind of prepared us slightly but gave us only a fleeting feeling of ease.

The questions were innocent, respectful, and in no way trying to catch us out. We initially thought that was exactly what was going to happen. All of the catching-out questions had been asked in the six months prior during our pre-approval training or ISW chats with Lyndsey. In comparison, all through the panel questions, we were literally on the edge of our seats answering the relatively simple queries. Do we think we're ready? How's Richard doing? What are your thoughts on children with disability? Even the inevitable question surrounding my caution, asked by the ex-policeman obviously, was relatively uncomplicated. 'How do you think the lessons learned from your police caution will make you a better foster parent?' Blimey, I wasn't expecting that. I was thinking I was going to be grilled in a dark room with a lamp shining in my face. Perhaps prodded with a sharp stick to see if I react aggressively. None of that happened, a little disappointing as the story may have been better. It was a room of genuinely lovely people making sure that we, too, were genuinely lovely people. Fifteen minutes later, we were asked to leave and grab a coffee while they converse. The freeze-dried coffee hardly had time to dissolve before we were called back in. I hadn't had time to respond to Robin's 'how do you think we did?' question before there was a knock on the kitchen door.

"We have had time to consider your application," the chair of the panel started the response. "Credit to your independent social worker, Lyndsey, there appears to be little we couldn't extrapolate from your Form F. We're delighted to let you know we will be supporting this application. A formal decision in writing will be following in the next couple of weeks.

Congratulations."

Yes. I cried – just a little. I don't think anyone noticed. It's a weird feeling, but for thirty years I knew I wanted to be a dad. I didn't know how and only nine months before this day, I was most of the way to getting an adopted child. Today, this day, twenty-fourth of April 2019, I found out I was going to be a dad. I'm not going to compare it to the feeling of finding out you managed to biologically produce an embryo as I will never know what that feels like. I will, however, tell you it felt awesome, a huge feeling of relief and joy. All in one go.

The drive home was relatively quiet to the drive there. I guess we were both contemplating the decision more than reacting to it. We started to talk about what kind of children we think will do well in our home. We settled on our make believe four-year-old twins, one boy and one girl, who need a warm, safe, caring home that we can spoil with shopping trips, football practice, and any other socially stereotypical pastime we could think of. We told our mothers immediately, and the same conversation was had again, and again. What children do we expect? When will we know? What are we going to do next?

10

24 April 2019 – Referrals

As soon as our panel had finished, one of the referral team had asked to see us. We hadn't even left the building. I had a bottle of Prosecco on ice at home with our names all over it. That was quick, we thought. We had plenty of questions about referrals. What do they look like? What kind of information is included? Do we have to accept the first one available? What do other carers do? We were also a bit on cloud nine, trying to hide our emotions, and a little excited. This meeting was just a catch-up to discuss with us in person what we said we were happy to take responsibility for. We had ticked zero to eighteen and every box on the list apart from heavily disabled as our house is not designed to cope with a wheelchair or slings.

It started with, 'Are you sure?' Why wouldn't we be sure. It felt a little like we were having our integrity questioned. After six months of, albeit very pleasant, interrogation, we wanted to just pick up a child now and go home. We had visions of a catalogue of cheeky faces, and you just pick what you want to come live with you. There is a sensible reason, however, in the question that was being asked of us. Apparently, many foster carers are rather restrictive. Probably the reason for the list I guess. It would have been easier if there was a box that said, 'Do you want to help young people no matter the situation?' I can understand some situations that would call for consideration of certain beliefs. For example, a staunchly Christian foster family taking on a staunchly Muslim child would be counterproductive. You'd like to think, however, that to have the gumption to become a foster parent, you'd be rather open-minded. However, a foster parent refusing a child because of a history of incest for example because they couldn't handle that emotionally doesn't quite make sense to me. Your job is to deal with emotionally challenging situations, we'd had all the training. Designed probably to scare off those carers who can't or won't deal with the really challenging behaviour that you will experience in your foster career. Incest isn't a pleasant conversation subject for anyone, but it doesn't mean you get to turn a blind eye because it doesn't match your values. Newsflash, it doesn't match any peoples' values. Knowing what we know now, and experiencing what we have, it makes sense that some carers would want a slightly quieter life and perhaps not tick the autistic, ADHD, PTSD, or Down's syndrome boxes. Even though we have learnt what we have during our time, we'd still take all the above, that's just our nature.

As you go through the list of questions, as we were now doing in person, they do make you wonder about your own values in life. Are you as liberal as you think? We thought that we would be happy with anything. Autistic children, no problem. Ethnic minority, easy. History of sexual abuse, umm, bit more serious but we can handle it. It's difficult questions like these that can really test your resolve. We had just got out of a meeting where we promised to show resilience and understanding. How could we now say we're not prepared to look after the needy. It would counter our promise. We hesitated a few times but always came out with the same decision. If the child was suitable, we would be happy to take any of them. Even seriously disabled children if the local authority were willing to invest in our property to provide a safe home for them. I got quite excited by the prospect of learning about different cultures. I certainly do not have a problem taking a Muslim child to a mosque for their weekly prayers. I'm not sure how the mosque would react to gay dads dropping off their Muslim foster child, but that's their issue. The issue is, would *we* have a problem with it? The answer is certainly not.

Then there is the other side of the coin. Not only do we need to match our own values and standards with a child, but the child needs to match with us. Perhaps a child of a certain religious faith has outright refused to be looked after by same sex parents. That's okay. Perhaps even the social worker is adamant that a relationship of such disparity would never work.

That's okay too.

It would need to work both ways to be a successful placement anyway. We wouldn't want a child to be forced to live with us against their consent, that's a sure recipe for an early disaster. With that in mind, we must write our own little summary of who we are and what we're about. A brochure of sorts, with nice photos of us, our family, and the house we live in. Luckily for us, our house is looking smart after my summer of refurbishments. I've also got a pretty cool motorbike, which turns heads and impresses the grumpiest of child at the flick of a switch. It's a bit weird writing a marketing brochure for your life. It feels a little shallow, but we understand its necessity. I remember cringing at the first version as it looked a little Microsoft Publisher-esque and not the type of professional document I'm used to. In the grand scheme of things, though, I imagine social workers around the country receive thousands of these on a weekly basis. The last thing they are worried about is the colour chart used for the background layouts. Perhaps the kids will be more forgiving, or will their expectations be higher? After all, this generation coming through school is more technically advanced than most adults for sure.

We thought we would be capable and happy to take on any child and were quite happy saying yes to pretty much any referral we got. If we say 'yes' to them all, one is bound to stick, right? We were warned that initially not all the referrals will be relevant. The 'No's' are just as important as the 'Yes's'. It gives the referral team a better understanding of the children we would be prepared to look after. We're still pretty confident we would look after all of them. They did ask one interesting question, too.

"Do you want photos?"

We agreed that it should be a blind placement. I certainly don't want to be held accountable for favouritism in decision-making based on appearance. Also, I don't want to get attached to a photo if a placement doesn't go ahead. One of our first referrals was young twins, one with spina bifida, how could we say no. Sister girls, with a history of abuse, were going through court for removal this week and needed to know if we could take them. If successful, we would need to be ready immediately. Within seconds, I was scouring the shades of Farrow and Ball Pinks to see what colours we were going to paint the bedrooms. Another of the first referrals we got was rather detailed, which we obviously wanted to read. It's compelling, even if disturbing, to read the histories of some of these children. This particular referral was a mixed-race boy, nine-years-old to very religious parents. The parents had very separate religious beliefs and one had schizophrenia. I have no idea how the social system hasn't dealt with this better, it goes to show how strained the system is not to have removed this child before now. The child had injured a previous carer quite badly and was obviously very angry with life. We said no, not because we didn't want to help, but the help this child needed was completely beyond our capabilities for a first official placement. We needed a slightly softer start. Local boroughs have to exhaust every possible opportunity they can with a child in care, including our own specialist therapeutic care. What that child needed was a secure home, a residency where medical professionals are on hand day and night. This service costs upwards of five thousand pounds a week, so any council worth their salt is going to try every avenue possible before signing off that expense. Unfortunately, some situations are still driven by cost and value.

We realised very quickly that we were now part of the system. The system we had complained about so bitterly when it came to the services afforded to Richard. We would have to deal with the political and financial motivations of all parties from within, not just look on from the outside and criticise. We were the system – part of the solution, not the problem.

The referrals kept coming, one after the other. Sometimes we would wait a week and nothing. Sometimes we would get three or four in a day and would react so quickly, just in case another carer snapped them up. At times it felt like a meat market and other times it felt like the advertised shortage of carers didn't exist at all. We picked up the phone several times to our new Supervising Social Worker (SSW), asking if they had missed our details on the call sheet. Weirdly stressful times not even having a placement, what were we going to be like with a child in our care?

11

2 June 2019 – Our First Placement

Robin received the message from the referrals team one afternoon while I was at work. They needed an emergency two-week respite placement for a boy called Lucas.

"We're sending over his documents now but need an answer quickly, he's going into residential care as he's not compatible with any of our carers and has had a number of failed placements. These include suicidal thoughts and actions. He's violent, a runner, and a biter. He will be with you for two weeks on respite."

The referrals team are always short in their approach as the business of placing, finding and referring kids in social care requires speed over politeness. The call came at the same time as the referral email, these guys are good. Robin responded on both of our behalf.

"Yes, of course we will take him."

We felt that a short two-week placement of an obviously challenging child could be the kickstart we need. Do well with this one and they'll be queuing up, we thought. It didn't matter that we would need to 'stag-on' all night to make sure he doesn't get up to any mischief. I spent twenty minutes explaining what 'Stagging On' – a military term – meant and at the same time promised not to use any more military terminology to manage a child in care with us again. Basically, it's working in short shifts overnight to monitor what's going on.

This was it, the first time a child in care was moving in to be looked after by us. The excitement, replaced by despair later, of reading all the referrals was now moving quickly into anxiety.

"What if he doesn't like us? What if he tries to hurt himself?"

We had read his rather detailed history now and some of the reports from previous carers did not hold him in the best of light. He had an issue with knives to the point of unsuccessful attempts to take his own life. He resorted to violence and aggression as a first response, including injuring a previous carer. The thought of a young person who isn't our blood or kin staying over for two weeks in our charge was a big thing for us. We had had our three-year-old nephew and twelve-year-old niece over for a week in the summer and were exhausted after that. Let alone two weeks, which on paper sounded like it was going to be a bit of a handful. We doubted we were even ready – my mind was racing.

"We will be fine. We've had all the training we need."

I was trying to console myself *and* convince myself probably more than Robin.

"Sod it, it's two weeks. Can't be any worse than Richard!"

I was trying to be the brave one here.

The first visit was from his social worker, who came alone to scope us out. She had been with him since the start of his care at the age of seven, he was now eleven. She wanted to come down and take some more photographs. I think she wanted to meet us to see if we would fit his personality and gauge our experience. She was obviously very protective over him. You could sense the level of ownership she had over the care of Lucas. It was refreshing to hear from a social worker who was so personally involved as our experience so far was limited to Richard's social workers, who were far from helpful. We had also heard the horror stories from other foster carers about uninterested social workers or the fact that it can be a rather transient industry. With social workers moving from one job to another, some children can feel even more anxious over attachments. Reading the history of Lucas, it was obvious to us that his attachment issues revolved around his desire to be around his birth family. Anyone who was part of the reasons for that not happening was the enemy. We were not surprised that he had issues being moved from his home to nearly ten other homes in the space of four years. You'd expect him to be a little unsettled. Now he was moving into yet another, such a trying time for him at such a young age.

He hadn't been told he was going into residential care, and we agreed to continue with the decision to not tell him quite yet. The thought was to let us give him some calm before he moves into his permanent residency. His social worker agreed with us that a period of rest would be good for him. As far as he was concerned, he was being taken to another care home yet again, and from what we understand, there were several tears and tantrums in the process. Quite understandably so. I'm not sure opening the car door and attempting to jump out on the motorway was an acceptable level of tantrum, but it wasn't unexpected considering his report. His social worker called us on the way to explain why they were a little delayed. I can't even start to imagine what that it is like for him. All I knew was that our house was a safe space and we were going to make it as fun as possible. His first week was planned with military precision. Cinema, football in the park, and a weekend at a theme park. The theme park I just happen to be a director of, so it comes with many behind the scenes perks. What kind of eleven-year-old wouldn't like that? When he arrived at the house, I was still at work, so Robin had the pleasure of welcoming him to our home. His social worker was on hand to assist, and rumour has it he whispered to her, 'Well done, good choice.' One of those heart-melting moments – we'll take what we can get at this point. She decided to just leave him and not make it a big thing. Just a cursory wave and glance, hoping that if he didn't notice too much it would be less painful.

When I got home, Lucas was watching television with Robin. I got a very polite and confident welcome into my own home. A firm handshake and an adult-like introduction.

"So, you must be Larry."

He had the cheekiest face and a smile as wide as his head.

"So, you must be Lucas."

He and I were anxious to ask plenty of questions. The small talk that he was obviously quite used to, and I was bumbling my way through my first attempt. Food, hobbies, likes, and dislikes. I wanted to get the full lowdown. Robin prepared some beige food, always a winner on day one we thought, while Lucas and I went outside to build the new football goal we had bought in preparation.

Lucas, I found out, was an avid football fan and was so very excited to have a kick about. He seemed to support whatever team came into his head, Manchester United is a safe bet. I am not a brilliant footballer or supporter so reverted to confirming that was my dad's favourite team. I had dropped a clanger in our first five minutes talking about my own dad to a kid who doesn't have any positive male role models in his life, let alone a dad. The only men in his life he is aware of bring thoughts that remind him of abusive relationships and memories. I'd screwed it up already.

"Don't worry, I'm not going to blame you for talking about your dad."

His adult like approached to everything was staggering. At this time, he moved on to claiming, "No-one has ever done this with me before."

Spending time building goal posts in the garden so we could have a kick around was apparently new to him in many ways. I foolishly thought that kicking a ball about with an eleven-year-old was foster parenting 101. It surprised me that, in nearly ten homes and four years, no-one had had the same thought to do this with him. Was this a test? Was he telling me porkies within the first hour? Was he just tugging at my heart strings to gauge a reaction from me? This boy is either very clever or I'm over-thinking this whole process.

"Why would anyone not want to do this?" I asked.

He shrugged.

It doesn't require a degree in social sciences to realise that sport and running around are good elements to combine on day one. There is, however, the very real possibility he is making this story up, too, for compassionate reasons. I was, however, sure this would reduce some barriers and get over the first day nerves. We played till it got dark and we completely lost track of the time and our impending hunger. Robin had finished dinner forty-five minutes earlier but did not want to disturb our so far successful foster carer/foster child start to our relationship. Towards the end, I did cheat a little bit and resorted to tickling as a tackling tactic. He did not appreciate it and whether it was because I scored or because it was a genuine invasion of his privacy, he duly told me off.

"I do NOT like being tickled."

The fear that I have definitely ruined day one overwhelmed me. If it wasn't my comparisons with my real father and his lack of one, I was sure this was going to result in a complaint against me for physical abuse. Day one is a learning curve like no other. When, or if, you have your day one, you will realise. We had so much to catch up on and so little time to work out each other's boundaries. As it turns out, I thought maybe someone in his past had tickled him to a point of making him feel endangered. Perhaps he associated the feeling of helplessness with a good tickle, or even to one of total vulnerability. I was supposed to be making him feel safe, not vulnerable. The very idea that I had somehow reminded him of a historic abuser filled me with dread. When I explained this to the team at the agency, I was also reminded that this is often the first action of many a paedophile. This did nothing to reduce my panic around the situation at all.

After dinner, I questioned the moral obligations of permitting twelve-rated films to be shown to an eleven-year-old in care. I lost the argument, secretly thankful as I was yet to watch the latest Avengers movie. This led into bedtime, which wasn't easy, but we managed it. We had known from his report that bedtimes were a real challenge for him. Perhaps it was something in his past, but really it was because he suffered greatly from nightmares, and he associated sleep with nightmares. Lucas was adamant that I needed to read to him each night, I had found Revolting Rhymes by Roald Dhal in the attic the previous week in preparation for such a moment. To my stupefaction, I hadn't realised Roald Dahl described Cinderella as a 'slut', be warned parents who dig out this book. When in full swing of the rhyming wildness of Mr Dahl, I couldn't remove the word or change it to something else with the speed required for a good bedtime read. I just sped up instead and I think I got away with it. I haven't yet, to this day, had to explain why Cinderella was described as a slut in a children's book.

He obviously had issues with sleeping in a new bedroom, in

a new house. This, together with his general dislike for sleeping and bedtimes, made it challenging but not impossible. He eventually fell asleep in our house – being looked after by us. Another milestone in our journey as foster parents. I can't help but keep a visual memory of this incredibly vulnerable but cute sleeping child in our home. Safe, secure, and sleeping soundly. I went to stroke his head and move his hair from his eyes as he slept just one last time before I leave him, then hesitated, trying to remember all my training. What did they say about physical contact? Is it permitted to stroke hair whilst they're sleep?

What a dilemma, what a drama. I did it anyway and he let out a little sigh of contentment, or he was winding me up. One of the two, but I'm going with satisfied sigh.

The next week was a rapid learning environment for all of us. Lucas had issues at bedtime but, aside from that, was generally a normal eleven-year-old. He liked beige food, farting, strumming his guitar, and asking a lot of 'why' questions. Bedtime was his biggest challenge as we understand now that the abuse he received in his early years happened around bedtime, in the bedroom, or while he was asleep. Needless to say, he hated being put to bed. I would spend an hour convincing him that he was safe, reading a book, talking about stuff, then eventually watch him drift off. I'd tuck him in, whisper some form of calming 'sleep well little one' and leave. Maybe stroke his head. Robin had a much better approach, which included making him read the book himself until he fell asleep, usually within ten minutes. Needless to say, Robin took over the bedtime routine.

He would constantly tell us that he had nightmares in the morning, and you can't help but sympathise. Poor boy, such a troubled start to life must be hard. So, we bought him a dream catcher.

"Doesn't work!' he said.

It didn't, he was right, and he would be restless most evenings. I don't think he had the nightmares he was imagining he had as we would watch him sleep, lightly, but he was sleeping. However, each morning he would make the same complaint. He would also wake sweating and certainly didn't look like he'd had a good, deep sleep. One evening, I went in to switch off his bedside lamp. The switch was enough to wake him from his light sleep and the look of pure terror on his face was heart-breaking. He shot up and out of bed to the other side of the room, white as a sheet, cowering in the corner. I had inadvertently startled him, and he was quite possibly reminded of his darker days before care. I hated myself for that. I desperately tried to reassure him with shushes and calming words, which probably didn't help. Why do we even say 'There, there'? It really did drive home to me some of the emotions he must be feeling in a new home with new, strange men in his bedroom. It has stayed with me to this day, the emotions and behaviours of looked after children are so wildly varied and change on a penny.

Three days later, during the morning routine of gently waking him, he arose with that cheeky-faced wide smile of his.

"It worked, it really worked. I didn't have any nightmares. I can't believe it actually worked."

The reference to our dreamcatcher actually doing its job for once.

"You can have your dreamcatcher back, I don't need it any more."

Psychologists will tell you more about his actions than I will pretend to understand, but we were proud nonetheless. We had achieved something good for him. I do know that the significance of beating his nightmares and handing back the dreamcatcher was his way of being settled one more step in his placement with us. He was comfortable with us, with the house – with the situation. Whatever it was, it certainly felt good to us to be involved in his recovery as a child with issues. Helping him transition from a scared, tired, and distant little boy to a happy, sleepy child dreaming of puppies and butterflies.

After nine days, we were really enjoying his company. The thought of him going to a residential home was heart-breaking. He was such a playful, cheeky, and engaging child, we couldn't let him be condemned to a life without the love of a home and a family. We wanted him to experience the home we had created, not go to some secure facility that, in essence, may suck any life left out of him. We had obviously conjured up Oliver Twist-esque pictures of what a residential home looks like. I'm sure it's not as bad as we thought. What I was certain of was that it didn't include us, and we were doing a pretty awesome job so far. We had not experienced much of the behavioural traits we had been warned about.

Everyone talks about the honeymoon period with young people, but that's not the case with Lucas, unless I'm still in it. He tested our resolve several times and, yes, threatened to hurt himself, as his background suggested. We dealt with it in our own way. We ignored his tantrums, didn't react to his tests, and called his bluff on his dramatic threats. We found it difficult to believe that he would run away when we could see him on our external security cameras sitting in the driveway. We also knew he would never drag that massive suitcase down the gravel driveway. All it served was as a nice distraction from our quiet cup of tea and a source of entertainment from the wireless camera. We knew he was safe from threatening to throwing himself out of his bedroom window when there are locks on them. Instead of pandering to his cries for attention, we just carried on drinking our tea and chatting. Which temporarily made his tantrum worse, which we also ignored. What it taught him is that he is safe. Not only is he safe with us, but we didn't require testing to demonstrate our desire to care for him. Despite him telling us we were terrible foster parents, failed all his tests, and he hated us. We just carried on.

A fostering colleague of ours has a sibling group of four. Some of the stories perhaps make me grateful now not to have followed suit in this endeavour, which was our original dream set up. We all got on well during our skills to foster training, where she represented a sounding board for prospective parents from the experienced foster parent position. Our relationship instantly took off as we shared similar values. We remained in contact and even met for lunch. It was nice to continue the relationship where we could moan honestly with each other about the pitfalls of the 'job' and the challenges that you wouldn't feel comfortable sharing with a social worker for fear of sounding negative. We would text about the progress of Lucas. Our first placement was hot topic and I wanted to share the journey. She was intrigued and enjoyed giving us advice. In the beginning of the placement, and as we shared the experience, she asked us if we liked him. Was it important that we liked him? As a respite placement on his way to residential, perhaps we didn't want to like him. We may well have been trying hard not to like him. Her advice was that, if we liked him, fight for him. Part of our job as foster carers was to advocate for our child in care. If we thought that residential wasn't suitable for him, and that we could offer him an alternative, we should fight for him. After all, we are now the professional parents and our views and assessment of the situation matters just as much as any other member of the team around the child. We can always be told we're wrong – worst case scenario.

That evening, we talked about whether we thought Lucas was a good fit for us and our household. We talked about how we thought he was doing and our retrospective feelings towards him. We did like him; we did want to fight for him. He has a solo placement order on him, so fighting for him now means we wouldn't get a second child for a long time, if ever. Something that we really didn't want to do. The problem is, we were besotted with this little man and couldn't see him progressing as well in a residential care as he could with us. The very next day, we called our own supervising social worker to discuss the situation. Even over the phone, we could tell she was rolling her eyes at us.

"I knew this would happen, I told the girls in the office 'they're going to want to keep him!' and I was right," she said.

We did want to keep him, and we discussed the next steps of what we needed to do. Lucas' social worker was about to tell him about residential care. She said she would break the news to him today after school. We asked her politely if she would hold on to listen to what we have to say.

Janet, Lucas's social worker, was keen to understand why we were so keen on keeping him here with us. Janet, remember, was the one we were really impressed with. The one who had been a constant in Lucas' life and the one adult in his life who had been there for him time and time again. Were we sure? We had never been more sure about something. Giving Lucas a home was all we wanted to do. He obviously needed a fresh start and clean slate. We were patient, found most of his antics funny, and were building a lasting relationship with him. More to the point, we flat out asked him if he was happy and wanted to stay with us.

Everyone was in agreement – us three boys and the army of professionals that surrounded us. Not only did everyone agree, but we were all much happier for it. Lucas was told about this being his final placement and a permanent placement until he's eighteen. He had gotten to terms with never returning to his biological mum. Coming to terms with and understanding why are two very different things. He was, we believe, relatively happy with the alternative.

One thing that was particular about us that other placements didn't share was that we were two men. Lucas has an issue with mother figures replacing his own mother. He's very proud and protective of his own mother and loves her so very much. Any woman that tries to 'mother' him is instantly rejected, sometimes violently. With us, that just wouldn't and couldn't happen. Neither of us could ever replace his mum because, biologically, we just didn't fit the bill. For an eleven-year-old, the stereotype of a mother is not covered by Robin, who it turns out definitely is the one who mothers him. What I could fill was his need and desire for a positive male role model in his life. Both my husband and I have different personalities and roles in the family. Robin is the stay-at-home dad, preparing lunch boxes, doing washing, chatting about soap operas, and getting his mani-pedi done on the odd treat day. I am 'go to work' dad. I wear suits, go to work, come home, and talk about my day. I bring the boy to work with me sometimes as a treat and he gets a kick out of saying 'my dad works here'. It's two very different roles and Lucas deals with us both differently. What he doesn't treat us like is a replacement for his mum. We talk about his mum quite a bit. We also talk about how we can never and would never replace her. We put positive behaviour and contact with his mum in the same box. This encourages good behaviour, ensuring that his contacts are always about positivity. If we associated tantrums or being upset with calling his mum, it would have the opposite effect. All we're doing is getting him through the first part of his life as best we can, making sure he is the best version of himself he can be.

As Lucas is a seasoned child in care, ten placements in four years, he's got the language down pat. He would talk about 'child in care' or 'team around the child' with natural ease. It's a little upsetting for us to hear such a young person talk this way as we want his life to be as normal as possible. We also didn't know as much of the lingo or acronyms as he did, which was rather embarrassing. We wondered what he would call us to other people as he goes through life. I'm sure it will change as we go. Foster carers sounds so formal and a little derogatory towards Lucas. He says he's fine with it but calling us his carers sounds weird to us. Foster parents is more our style and remains true to our professional parenting strategy. I think secretly that foster dads would be our favourite, mine anyway. The social recognition of a dad is, in my mind, higher up the hierarchy. My emotions are always a little on the surface anyway, so I'm pretty sure I'd lose control of them if he ever called me his dad. As I write this, his current favourite description is foster gays. We find the term endearing as we know it's not used in a derogatory nature. He can run around the kitchen in a superman pose chanting 'foster gays!' as if it's a type of superhero calling. He makes me laugh.

The clarity of his association with our roles was made wonderfully clear to us one morning when we were having this discussion about how to introduce us to other people and how he would like to be introduced to people by us. Over a slice of peanut butter on toast, he gave us the best reference to our identities I've ever heard. He explained to me that I don't look gay, which I can understand. Therefore, I was the 'Straight Dad' and Robin was the 'Gay Dad'. Which I also find funny. The social workers found it a bit weird, but we told them we find it endearing as opposed to offensive. I am not a stereotypical gay-looking person. On the other hand, a blind man with a cold can tell Robin is gay from five hundred yards. This brought on an interesting conversation about stereotypes. I was a volunteer role model for Diversity Role Models, a London charity which challenges stereotypes in the LGBTQ+ community. So, I had a whole speech set to memory for this conversation. Although the speech was written specifically for young people, I think he switched off as soon as I started on my routine. It reminded me of another training course I was on around mentoring and coaching roles in business. The one piece of advice I was given that I remember vividly was, 'Do not try these techniques on your family.' I can confidently attest to the further advice of, 'Do not lecture your family from a learnt script.' It is fact, however, that Lucas is quite proud of having two gay foster parents. We have been through a number of different scenarios with him about what to call us and how to act in public. It's nice to know he is relaxed and comfortable enough to be able to joke with us, have fun, and still be respectful.

We had noticed, however, that he would never be affectionate or officially be recognised in public as our child. Or rather, it took a very long time in comparison to the affection he would show at home. At home, he would insist on a cuddle before bed. Another in the morning before school. Out in public, it's a very different story. Whether it was as a looked after child or as biological offspring. He wouldn't introduce us to friends as anything other than his foster parents. It wasn't until I was helping him with his Science homework that, for the first time, he let us be acknowledged as an important parental position within his life. The homework was to create a vlog or presentation on the different things that happened in the process of cooking. Cooking just happens to be my thing, so I obviously completely took over the homework and set about creating a master piece video presentation on his behalf. One of the animated titles said, 'My dads didn't help me at all!' I was being a little risky, but when I presented it to him in video format, he was so happy that he didn't want to change a thing. I asked him specifically about this title and that it was easy for me to delete it or change it to carers, for example. He was happy, not only for us to be labelled as his dads, but for it to be broadcast to his friends at school. Considering that he had only just started in senior school, and bullying is rife at that age, I found it very brave of him. I feel a little guilty that I had pushed my own agenda onto him, but we wanted him to feel proud of us too. We wanted him to feel like it isn't a bad thing to tell people he's looked after by two guys. He shouldn't feel ashamed or embarrassed. I'm fully aware that being a looked after child is hard enough work for any young person to have to deal with but having gay dads on top must be nerve-racking. I'm also aware that his generation tend not to give two hoots about the LGBTQ+ community. Every young person has a gay uncle or aunt nowadays. It's a bit boring.

I failed the science homework – not happy about that. Apparently iMovie is not an authorised medium as a presentation.

For now, Lucas is settling in well and his attachment issues with his mum have not manifested into more serious actions or reactions with us. His history would show that he has issues with firm female figures trying to 'mother' him. Without that worrying us, we realised that we do still need to include women in his life and part of his development and treatment will be for him to manage those emotions. So, we purposefully looked out for female role models. Our neighbours are our nominated adults. This means they have been background checked and act on our behalf if we can't be there to look after Lucas for some reason. Caz has mothered two boys quite successfully with different challenges, one with physical ailments that has meant a lot of trips to the hospital and one with more challenging learning behaviours. She is more than qualified to deal with both Lucas' behaviour and to be a sounding board for us on our parenting techniques. Being so involved means we have that female interaction which we all agree is important for Lucas' mental growth. His swimming instructor is female, as is his martial arts instructor. Our own mothers, our friends, our sisters, and numerous child care professionals who grace our doorstep are welcomed to add that feminine touch to the developing mind of Lucas.

The argument that a child requires both female and male involvement to grow as rounded person is valid. It does not, however, need to be full time. For us, our rights as single sex male carers supersede the quite sensible aforementioned argument. We also happen to agree with the argument and think that women play a vital role in a young person's upbringing. I'm pretty certain, in our little myriad of adults that are involved in our life, Lucas has more women, varied in their nature, doting over him on a daily basis than many eleven-year-old boys do from a natural upbringing. Not one of them, in addition, is trying to be his mother – which he quite likes.

Our first major challenge in our care of Lucas came around school. It wasn't Lucas that was the problem, it was the team around him. Unlike some foster carers, we are not complacent, and we welcome all the professional help we get. I can say this from a point of experience and understand not all experiences are the same. I've refused to go to feedback meetings with our agency because it's all negative and I don't need that in my life. Whoever said a feedback meeting has to be negative? What about all the good they do? Our relative experience with Richard and the complete lack of support has made us very grateful of any support we get from the system and agency. Lucas was very upset when he found out he was leaving the area he had been in for the past two years. He had made new friends and although he clearly didn't get along as well with his previous foster carers, he had formed attachments with them and the security of that was once again being removed. For this reason, we did not consult him on the choice of new school. It was also a senior school as opposed to primary, which was a huge move for him. I remember the day I moved to secondary school, and it was certainly emotional. For him, however, the sense of loneliness must have been greatly more so than my own. To move schools, area, home, and a change of carers. No wonder he was prone to an emotional outburst or two.

We were presented with a number of schools to choose from and, as his primary carers, it was up to us, with the involvement of all the TAC (Team around the Child). This included the district school secretary, supervising social worker, Lucas' social worker, their supervisor, and the school district from his home district. It was a little overwhelming. The list of schools we were presented with did not have our first choice on it. We had found a school, with help from our local community, that would be perfect for Lucas. It had incredible pastoral care that was second to none in the area. We were convinced that he would be perfect there. It was a cycle ride from home, he would make friends in the local area, and it had a reputation for dealing with children in care very well. We insisted that the TAC applied to this particular school for us as we believed it would be perfect. We were told they were full, and he could not get in. We're not ones to sit idly by and be told we can't have something. We pushed and pushed, but nothing. We were sent one school twenty miles away with a pretty ropey reputation, another under-performing school, according to OFSTED, and two schools for children with learning difficulties. Lucas was two years behind his age, not because he has learning difficulty, it's because of being moved from pillar to post, not because he had learning disabilities of any kind. He was smart, articulate, kind, generous, and keen. We felt that we were the only ones fighting for him. Even our favourite of the social workers, Janet, appeared to have given in to ease as opposed to what was best for Lucas.

We had none of it and called the school ourselves. We wrote to the headmaster and insisted that he give us a chance and a meeting. Considering this was the last day of term before summer holidays, we had a fight on our hands. We wanted Lucas at this school. We learnt that Lucas had actually never been put on the list, we had not been rejected or accepted. We were furious. We arranged a meeting at the school, called the headmaster, invited the whole TAC, and in just one day before school closed for the summer, we had a rather heated meeting. Our disappointment in the system for letting down this child was known to everyone by the end of the meeting. District supervisors were put in their place and my patience for their bureaucracy was at zero. If it wasn't for Robin and I fighting tooth and nail for Lucas, he would not be in the place he is now. The headmaster agreed to admit him, and the TAC had no choice but to vote in favour. We left the meeting exhausted, but our own social worker came up to us and congratulated us on doing what many wouldn't. We fought for our looked after child as if he was our own. Somehow Lucas, who wasn't there, knew how hard we fought. He knew from then that we were the ones who were going to have his back for the rest of his young life. The echoes of that 'experienced carer' from our pre-fostering training repeated in my mind, 'If you like him, fight for him.' And the advice from the Army Cadet, 'Don't do it just for the money, we can always tell.'

I wrote to the headmaster recently, thanking him again for taking on Lucas, he didn't have to. I wanted to tell him what an improvement he had made under his leadership. That he was reacting well to whatever strategies and tactics he was implementing in his school. He replied and, to my surprise, knew only too well of Lucas' improvements and that he was a valued member of the school. I don't believe he knows all twelve hundred kids at his school, but I'm going to pretend he does, and I'll take his thanks to me for lifting his spirits on that day as genuine.

12

January 2020 – Could We Have Two?

When we passed our panel to become foster parents, we were accepted for two children to live with us. We hoped for a sibling group, maybe even three, or twins. It was exciting to imagine this new group of young people in our house, filling it with joy, laughter, tears, tantrums, food fights, and more. We knew that we wanted more than one, that's for sure. So, to be accepted for two was great, knowing full well we could increase that to three in the future should we want to, and should we prove we can.

Lucas was a special child who had been described as high risk, with suicidal threats, problems with knifes, he was a 'runner', and made threats to life. Quite a serious collection of challenges that didn't bother us one bit. One of the elements of his placement was that he would need to be a solo placement. Being approved for two meant that he would need to bed block. This is a process whereby his social worker would need to approve double payment for us not to have a second child. In essence, they would pay for our approved second bed to remain empty. Not a problem for us, a bit of a warm up, and we get paid for it. It was an ideal situation. Lucas would get our undivided attention and we would get the income required to pay the mortgage and bills. The instruction was limited to six months, so we knew that at some point it would either be going so well we would get another one or so badly he would continue to bed block.

We trialled the conversations with Lucas first with some leading questions.

"If you were to share us with another child, what would you want? Do you think it would be nice to have someone to play with?"

We toyed with the idea that a little sister might be nice. Robin would get to go girlie shopping and plait hair and Lucas would still be able to do boy stuff like football and martial arts with me. Lucas has a little sister, and we know he misses her dearly. It may be a great addition to our home to have a little girl, too.

"I want someone exactly my age who likes nerf gun wars," he said triumphantly, as if by saying it with such enthusiasm it would definitely make it happen.

Fresh from a nerf war myself, the thought of being ganged up on by two adolescent boys with plastic guns fills me with dread. Then again, I did want twins at one point. I have also spent a best part of twelve years in the army cadets, which is basically doing exactly that for most of the time.

The process of getting a second placement is not easy. There are a lot of adults in Lucas' life. His social worker, our social worker, psychiatrists, therapeutic carers, teachers, and then all of these people have supervisors that check up on the people checking up. All of these people have to be in agreement for a change in the child's life to take action. Only then can we even think about looking at referrals again to find a match.

The idea of parent and child came from one of the supervisors at the agency. More learning for us, what on earth is parent and child care? I wrongly assumed that it was mother and baby. Which, in essence, it is, however with the titles of parent and child, it doesn't take a scientist to work out that it includes men and their young children. Therefore my first reaction was that I didn't think it was a good idea. Lucas has issues with mother figures and a mother and baby may play havoc with our relatively calm house. On further discussions and being made aware it could be an adult male and young child, we were much more engaged. Then came the stories, foster care seems to be full of stories. Some were designed to put you off, some were designed to encourage you. Stories of babies being left with the foster carers indefinitely as the parents are estranged. One of a fifty-five year old man and a new born that did not end happily. Many stories of how hard it is to not get involved as this time is supposed to be for the birth parent to bond with their child in the safety of secure home environment with professionals on hand.

We set about with the further training we needed, alterations to the house, too. We needed car seats, cots, changing tables, and a myriad of other baby equipment in order to care for an infant. Not that we were the ones doing the caring, that was up to the natural parent. We were there for support, security, and safety. We could obviously lend a hand and you just try and stop me stealing a snuggle. I imagined some stressful late nights that we could make easier for the biological parent. My answer, as with most things I do, was of course yes. Robin was the main carer, so it was really up to him. He, too, liked the idea. He is usually the sensible one so, if he agrees, I'm happy with it.

The deal was that eighteen weeks of uninterrupted care was required. At the end of the eighteen weeks, the pair are reassessed. A decision would then be made on the suitability of the parent, their situation, and relationships with the child. If successful, I presume the agency will send them on their merry way under supervision of a local authority. If unsuccessful, the young child would be left with us, the parent would be sent on their way, and a suitable long-term solution would be sought. In order for us to provide uninterrupted care for eighteen weeks, we would need to avoid Christmas and February half term as during both those school holidays we had planned foreign travel. My job is incredibly demanding in the summer months, so we try to pack in a year's worth of family holiday in the few cold months of the year.

Great, this all sounds perfect, where do I sign.

Disaster – our social worker moves on. The thing we were warned about right at the beginning of our journey was happening. How on earth are we supposed to support and care for young people with consistency and security if we're constantly catching up with our own social worker. Six months of form F, pre care training, mandatory training, and two hundred days of report writing. Hours and hours of relationship building and hundreds of pounds of biscuits. Despite the other benefits and requirements of all of this, we had to start all over again with our new social worker. Annoying isn't the word. The sense of loyalty and responsibility we hold as foster parents, I can assure you, is not held by even the very best of social workers we met. Those ones get promoted! As a long-standing member of a youth group, I know only too well the demands of responsibility and loyalty to these young people.

I'm not one to moan or procrastinate. Our social worker must have found it terribly hard to move on from the many relationships she had built and her reasons, I hope, weren't too hard to overcome. I'm sure her reasons were honourable and valid. I wished her all the best. She was brilliant at her job and read us brilliantly. Our relationship was very natural and relaxed. We could talk freely and openly, and I missed that.

This could not be said for the next one. During our first chat with the replacement, I'm calling her Xena, she started to chastise us for Lucas missing one of his psychiatric assessments. Robin was not impressed. He's made every meeting and every appointment, and we've championed him at every moment. We have attended all the mandatory training, completed extra optional training, and beyond. I have a masters in youth leadership and, aside from caring for Lucas, Robin also volunteers as a Young Life Foundation carer. Should Xena have read our profile, she might have known all that and started with, 'Wow – aren't you guys doing well with Lucas. One thing I did notice, though, was a missed Psych test. Any reason for that?'

Instead we got, 'Psychological evaluations are expensive and missing one costs us money. Do not miss these please.' Well, that didn't start the relationship off very well that's for sure. Especially since we got on so well with the previous incumbent. I am extensively experienced and qualified in mentoring and coaching techniques. Alongside a number of management courses in getting the best out of people. My experience and qualifications give me the absolute right to pass comment that the approach she took was the opposite of how to do it. Building a relationship with people does not start with a telling off. Demonstrating ignorance through lack of research is insulting. It shows lack of empathy, lack of judgement, and a conscious decision to evoke a power play in the first instance. Not very therapeutic.

Fast forward three months and nothing has happened about the parent and child placement or any other placement for that matter. We had very little contact with our new social worker, and she hadn't even met Lucas yet. The decision had been made in our absence, through this handover, to prolong Lucas's bed blocking for at least another six months. There was a renewed level of focus on us at this time because our annual review panel is coming up. In preparation for that meeting, our current social worker decided to have a conference call, obviously conscious that spending three hours with us isn't enough to complete a full evaluation of our performance for the panel. She needs more info. In her normal curt manner, the meeting starts by telling us she doesn't think it's suitable for a parent and child placement as she doesn't believe it's best for Lucas and we're not experienced enough. This requires more detailed training. Completely different feedback from the last meeting and the training, which we had already received, is now not good enough.

My reply was something along the lines of, "Funny that, your agency are the ones who suggested we do it. The agency put us forward and recommended us for parent and child care. The agency, with our previous social worker, has completed some training with Robin. If this isn't enough, maybe we should have been told by the agency you represent."

"Oh," she replied.

After the conference call, I dialled back in to Robin.

As if I hadn't even caught a breath, I continued, "And another thing, she still hasn't even met Lucas. On what grounds is her assessment based. How dare she?"

There was more but I can't write it down here. I caught myself being a protective parent. Something carers are told to be careful of. These children in our care are not ours, they are looked after children and the surrounding team are all making decisions on our and their behalf. Although we must advocate for them at every opportunity and fight for them when no one else does. However, there are limits and we have to sometimes play to a different tune than we would if they were our own children. I often forget that, possibly to my own detriment.

Ten days later, our pre-panel meeting happened to discuss the reports everyone will be submitting with a manager from the agency. At this meeting, a supervisor came along to our house with Xena. We were diplomatic, polite, and followed our training. We mentioned not being bothered about parent and child, explained the misunderstanding, and quickly moved on to more positive elements. The care of Lucas who, by all accounts was thriving. He was no longer two years behind his peers at school. He was eating well, socialising, sleeping, and we'd had no signs of his challenging behaviour for months. Adults who knew of him over the past year, or years, of his care are genuinely surprised at the change. As I said before, and as we continue to get the same feedback, he is often described as a different child. Despite some of the negativity towards us by our new social worker, we were in their eyes a perfect match. A far cry from the deeply disappointing result we felt had happened with Richard. We used this as an example and described how the support network we now had was such a welcome addition to our lives as we have lived through caring for a special needs child without any support. Therefore we were also able to empathise with other parents who also had to deal with this kind of situation. It meant that we were also in an unusual situation to be both carer and to have experienced the process of going through struggling to manage a child.

We never discussed a second placement again after that pre-panel. We drifted from one base to the next and gently brought it up in casual conversation with Lucas and all our professionals from time to time. Four days after pre-panel, COVID-19 put the country in lockdown. This slowed down even the simplest of daily chores. It possibly made everything more complicated. Our panel was held remotely, it came and went quickly and painlessly. Nothing further was mentioned about a second placement.

A few weeks later, I received an email from Xena out of the blue telling us that she was instructing the referrals team to get in touch about a second placement. I couldn't believe it. It all felt rather unusual to the normal process, but I presumed it was a new COVID-safe thing. I replied and copied in the referrals team to my excitement in anticipation of a second placement. Finally, after so long being on our own with Lucas, we would be able to get a second placement. It was exciting, a new chapter, and a new challenge for us. With COVID-19 locking us all down, we thought that demand would be high to place children in care, so we thought we were doing our bit for the country. How very British of us. It didn't take long for all hell to break loose. At this point, we had apparently now been approved by the entire team for a second placement and I shouldn't have contacted the referrals team. Robin and I got a rather stern talking down from Xena over the phone about protocol and how I shouldn't get above my station. Pretty much a 'stay in your lane' chat. It didn't surprise me that she thought that was the appropriate way to talk to us. She hardly knew anything about us and, in my opinion, didn't understand the protocols herself, considering she was the one who started the email chain in the first place. We called management. We were not happy. We are possibly the easiest carers to manage and have been known to be laid back about many of the challenges we face in life and as carers. We're not difficult people. Until, of course, you call us and blame us for your own mistakes. Then that's a different matter.

We got a new Supervising Social Worker four weeks later, third one in under a year. Still no second child.

13

January 2020 – Dealing With the Issues

Lucas came with a lot of mental baggage as well as physical. His physical baggage was easy to handle. He explained to us that the two huge suitcases he burdened his entrance with hadn't been unpacked for possibly years. He didn't even know what was in them. He blamed his mean foster carers. We didn't believe him but turned it into a positive. When we got the go ahead to the request that he stays permanently, we told him that if we unpacked everything and spread it around the house, they would never be able to move him again because it would be too difficult. He loved this idea and took it upon himself to spread his belongings around the house with enthusiasm. It served to make the house feel like his home and helped him settle into his surrounding with ease. We both enjoyed the process immensely and celebrated our triumph with a rare pizza treat for lunch.

The unpacking party we reserved for his luggage unfortunately could not be applied to his emotional millstone. This manifests in a number of ways around his behaviour and how he reacts to certain situations. We were warned of his ability to run, for example. It was described in his referral documents that he has a tendency to run away. True to form, that's exactly what happened and very early on in his placement he decided, in his own words, to 'run away'. Possibly a learned term for storming out. He packed his bag, struggled his way down the stairs (the bag was bigger than him), and stormed out of the door, slamming the door shut behind him. Normally this act would result in his carers having to physically stop him and take control of the situation with relevant levels of arrest. However, luckily for us, the gravel driveway is not good for suitcases with wheels. He abruptly came to a halt, fed up with his fruitless labour, and sat on the suitcase in protest. We have a camera doorbell, so we watched the entire process on our phones while drinking tea in the back garden. He had no idea we could see him kicking stones, holding his head in his hands, and we could even see the general bemusement on his face while waiting for us to come flying out the door after him. We didn't, safely monitoring him from the comfort of our phones. After around fifteen minutes, he stormed back in into the rear garden.

"YOU ARE AWFUL FOSTER CARERS!" he proclaimed. "That was a test, AND YOU FAILED."

I don't think he expected us to laugh. He stormed out again, this time ensuring that the door was well and truly slammed shut. His second failed attempt to drag his heavy suitcase over the gravel was again a source for our amusement. Only ten minutes this time.

"That was a second test and you failed AGAIN! I'm going to report you to my social worker."

He was generally confused by our response. The perfect storm of gravel, security cameras, heavy suitcases, and a cup of tea made for a sharp lesson for him. The primary lesson was that he is safe here and running away is not an answer. Secondly, we are not going to pander him and run after him. He is in charge of his own destiny, and he needed to understand that. Within thirty minutes we were sitting down with a second cup of tea, hot chocolate for him, and we talked in detail about the reasons why he acted like that. It's vital that you ask the why, not deal with the situation. There is always a reason.

"Why do you feel the need to run away from a perfectly good home with two caring adults?"

Phrasing the questions in an open, friendly way paves for an open and friendly answer. He didn't know obviously, it's just what he knew. Don't like the situation, run away from it. At some point, a social worker will collect him and move him to the next environment.

Lucas wanted to test us. He wanted to find out how we would react. We reacted completely differently to other carers. Don't forget, the perfect storm enabled us to do that, not the fact that we're better than anyone else. The reaction he got from us wasn't to panic. To him we were relaxed about the whole thing. He didn't get the reaction he wanted. Either we were going to be tested even harder or we would fix the behaviour and he would change.

Suicidal thoughts, we believe again, were an action on his part designed to get us to intervene and react. His report included these as some tendencies, but we didn't really see any real threat in any of his actions. We believe he wanted to know how carers would react. He had issues with knives, so we had removed every single one from the house and locked them away. It wasn't until a few weeks in that he found a sharp steak knife in one of our hiding places. He was upset one day and came to us threatening to stab us. More a sense of being inquisitive as opposed to seriously threatening.

"What would you do if I stabbed you?" he asked, he had a knife and insinuated he wanted to stab me.

He was careful not to say kill himself or kill me, just stab, as this had brought more attention than he wanted the last time he had said something similar. Knowing his history, and understanding his behaviour, we decided to call his bluff. I asked him to stay still and wait for me to come back. This was the opposite of what he expected. I think he expected me to panic or wrestle him for the knife. I came back in the room with the first aid kit.

He asked me, "What's that for?"

I told him that I would need it to patch myself up if he stabbed me, hence the first aid kit. He was confused and told me that he would keep the knife and stab himself instead. I handed him the first aid kit – he was equally perplexed. We closely monitored him for the next thirty minutes, not letting him close his bedroom door so we could keep an eye on him. He realised that we were a worthy advisory to his games. After thirty minutes he gave up, came to us, handed us the knife, and apologised for his behaviour. We had given him the space, time, and resources to work out that his own behaviour was unacceptable. This whole process was designed for him to be able to self-regulate and come up with the solution himself. We did everything we could to protect him from getting into the situation in the first place. However, sometimes kids have a way, without you knowing what they're up to. We ensured he was safe and supervised at all times but didn't panic, didn't shout, or blame him for any of it. We didn't tell him he was a bad boy, or a dangerous person, or that we were frightened. We were calm – we believe that is what encouraged him to be calm in return. We used his threat, which was a test of his own safety, turning it around, and by not being hysterical, he realised we were the ones who would be able to trust him, show him love, and protect him for the rest of his childhood. The test was just in case the future throws up any big curve balls and to ensure that we would have his back. This proved we would. Is it text-book foster care? Certainly not. Would we do this again given our time over? No idea. What we do know is how to read the situation as it happens, no professional social worker would be able to tell us different, we saw it as it was. We saw Lucas for who he was, a scared little boy with serious attachment issues that just needed consistency in his life to overcome them.

It never happened again after that. We slowly started to reintroduce knives into the household, starting with the steak knives before moving to the bigger kitchen knives. He started to realise what was happening, and when he exclaimed in his awareness of the appearance of sharp objects again, we explained it was because we trusted him. His positive actions had positive reactions. Admittedly, we had a small hiccup and had to start the whole process over again. This did not deter us or make us think that the actions were in anyway incorrect because they hadn't worked the first time. Perseverance is one of the virtues foster carers must have in the practice of resilience. Not giving up is one of our values that we cherish. Not to say that, if the situation became unbearable, we won't look after ourselves first. It's just that not including it as an option makes us search harder for an alternative solution.

His violence was a muscle memory for him. When he got angry, he would involuntarily lash out, punch the air, or us if we were in his way. We would calmly stop him, explain what he's done, and ask him to think about not doing it next time. If we caught his hands in 'mid-punch', he would use his head. At three foot six inches tall, this would land squarely in my belly and remind me to lose weight more than anything else. If the belly headbutt move didn't give him the required reaction, he'd go with a kick, or knee, and even at his height, he was perfectly placed for the one weakness in a two-man relationship. The goolies, crown jewels, John Thomas, and any other colloquial reference to the unmentionables would be his last resort. He obviously wanted a reaction. This was the only way he knew how to get one. No fear of me losing the ability to have children was, I guess, albeit slight, a silver lining.

Over time, that ever-important theory of resilient-led therapeutic care can run thin. Being punched in the balls was not pleasant. We would challenge it every time, explain why it's not cool or beneficial. Every time he did it, he would lose a privilege, like using the iPad, watching TV, choosing dinner, or going out on his bike. Eventually you see his brain working through his facial expressions. When he got frustrated with a maths problem, his fist would clench but he would scream into his chest and then breathe himself out of it without hitting anyone. This is progress. Every now and again, he would still lash out. We would explain what went wrong and I explained that, if I feel low or down, I prefer to make myself better with a hug. We're huggers not haters in this house. Less anger, more love would be something I'd say a lot. He could lash out and headbutt my belly, then I'd say, 'less anger, more love'. He'd immediately say sorry, give me a hug, and get back to his maths problem. A mixture of improved behaviour and 'improving' behaviour was a win for us.

Now we are much improved, it did a take while. I still experience his clenched fists and he will even raise them at me sometimes. You can then see in his face that he realises what he's doing is wrong. He will stop himself without me saying anything at all. He will lower his arms, force them to his sides, and grumble. I know he can't help it, it's the reason why I don't react to it. If I reacted, he would get more frustrated. The fear will always be there as he grows up and gets stronger. The hope is we can teach the muscle reaction of violence out of him. In many of our academic books on therapeutic care or attachment, it will tell you that whatever is learned can be unlearned. We're hoping that his 'go to' response is a learned behaviour. Then we can put into place a process of unlearning it. Instead of reacting negatively to an aggressive situation, we use it as a learning experience and discuss what the right action would have been. I can only imagine what his aggression may be like coming from an angry sixteen-year-old. It fills me with dread that, if it does come to that, we are not qualified or prepared to tolerate regular physical abuse from someone who will or could cause serious injury. I gave up playing rugby as I got older due to the physical pressure it can add to your body. I don't particularly want to experience that again in my own home, thank you. We hope daily that all our hard work now will put us in good stead in the future.

Will he also have the restraint he has learnt so recently? When the teenage years kick in, will it be different? I guess we will have to see, and we will get through that challenge when we get to it.

One of his flaws is he has a natural desire to cheat, evade, and lie about his achievements. Not completely abnormal in an adolescent to avoid situations that may lead to disciplinary action by denying everything. However, his commitment to this action of his is staunchly consistent. I have experience of twelve to eighteen-year-olds for twelve years with the army cadets, but it is in the values and standards of all cadets not to lie, so this behaviour in young people is very new to me.

One of his worst moments was the theft of money from the house. I never really found out all the truth, but we caught him in the bank with foreign money. He was trying to change it into pound sterling. He had obviously been malicious in his actions. Theft from us was something we abhorred, and it was the only time I've got serious and been angry with him. In a controlled manner, of course, but my voice was raised, it was stern and unforgiving. It was one of those 'I'm disappointed' moments as opposed to 'I'm angry'. Although I was pretty angry. He has never done it since and I hope will never do it again. Teaching him about pocket money and the relative relationship with his needs to spend money helped. As he got older, his pocket money would increase with his needs. For now, six pounds a week for an eleven-year-old was plenty.

His lying is also relevant in the simplest of requirements. Cleaning teeth is the most challenging of pastimes. Not your normal environment of 'Did you clean your teeth', with the response of 'No, do I have to?' bookended with, 'Yes, do it now'. That would be a normal exchange of parent-child teeth cleaning issues. Lucas would go out of his way not to do it, pretend he did it, and then make his breath taste of toothpaste rather than do it to pass the breath-smelling test. Perhaps it is normal, we're not experienced enough to pass comment. I am acutely aware that his approach to homework is abnormal. Abnormal to me and my friends' children anyway. It would be hidden, ripped up, or thrown away before he even got home so he didn't have to do it. He would hide things away and pretend they never happened. It's unusually military in style in how he desperately tried not to do anything. When challenged, he would wince away and look scared. I'm worried that this reaction to be challenged is his way of 'getting away with it'. Surely no adult who knows his story could withstand the puppy eyes. You'd need to be a superhero to stand up to those big blues. Well, it just so happens that we had those super powers.

We tried initially by using softer words, like fibbing, tricking, or 'untruths'. Trying to use less aggressive language, giving him the confidence and courage to be honest. Teaching him that honesty is the best form because it shows strength of character [side note: it always makes me laugh when I talk about his strength of character. He's the strongest human I've ever met.

To have dealt with the challenges already in his life at such a young age]. We thought that focusing on positive language and a softer approach to consequences may encourage him to lie less (sorry, fib less). It didn't work, it took greater measures, so I handed the baton of discipline to Robin, the task master of our relationship.

We tried a different tactic, challenging the behaviour with instant punishment, deep discussion about cause and effect, and limited time periods to come clean – this was measured in seconds not minutes. Whereas before we would like him to go away and think about his actions and come back to us when he was ready to tell the truth. This time, he had to stand there and tell us the truth instantly, every second that passed resulted in another piece of electronic equipment, favourite toy, or treat being removed from this arsenal. When we ran out of things, we counted in days.

I believe that being in care for four years meant that he had managed to get away with different things with different carers. With us, he was finding out what he could get away with. It was nothing, by the way. He couldn't get away with anything when it came to us. He had met his equal, a noble adversary that matched his cunning. Years of reading the Beano was finally rewarding me. I think, because we were committed to keeping him till he was eighteen, we had a different approach than previous carers. We were hoping to set ourselves up for a future where we didn't have to deal with this type of behaviour for the next six years.

14

2020 – COVID-19

Our one-year panel was scheduled for early March 2020. The first death in the UK occurred on 28 February. Things changed very quickly from that date, and by the time our annual panel came, we were in full lock down and a conference call was the only real way it could be done. We certainly didn't want to delay or postpone the meeting as it may not have been rescheduled for months. Xena called us again to discuss the content. It all felt a little like a box ticking exercise. Singing from the same hymn sheet as last time the conversation felt a little repetitive, but we duly nodded our way through the conversation. We touched on the parent and child care process and my desire to be approved for a third child. We had a five-bedroom house and we bought it because we wanted to fill it with children. Our initial approval for two children was, we always thought, 'a start'. She also met Lucas and asked him to fill in a short questionnaire. The questions were around us and also her. He scribbled 'never met her' in most of the boxes and for us drew a picture of a happy family. Questionnaire done.

The virtual conference was not the same as I had imagined I'd be able to justify why I thought we were suitable for more than two. The panel was a very similar process as the initial one. The members included experienced carers, supervisors, social workers, and a chairperson. They all expressed that they were impressed with the progress of Lucas in our care, and I think we answered all the questions we needed to. In the early days of Lockdown 1.0, Zoom and Microsoft Teams were in their infancy, so telephone conference was the only option. Having it done remotely was very weird. Not seeing their faces let us make up our own versions of who was on the phone and we certainly didn't dress anywhere nearly as smart as we did at the first panel. Not sure if anyone has done a foster care panel in pyjamas before, until now. Not because we couldn't be bothered to get dress but, in the new lockdown, pyjamas was the new uniform of the day for all of us.

The lockdown was a very new experience for the entire planet. I went from working seventy to ninety hours a week to being home all week. Lucas was home from school, so the relative quiet days that Robin would enjoy Monday to Friday were over. Luckily for him, and my own sanity, we were here for each other so we could tag team the additional care required.

Initially, Lucas was invited back to school as he was in care and therefore considered a priority for the local authority to provide education to. We made the decision that, in actual fact, our responsibility was for him to be treated like any other child. That level of normality meant that he would be home-schooled like most of the other children in his class. This idea filled him with excitement and anticipation of bottomless hot chocolate break times, cuddles with the teachers, and not having to wear a uniform. He was correct on one front. Robin refused to iron any more uniforms.

Initially, we tried Robin playing the part of teacher. I think his patience for education was shorter than mine for some reason. The lessons were unproductive and, being the very first time this remote form of education was being used, Robin also had to deal with teething issues from the school's side too. Lucas got expelled from the school of Robin on his first day and was sent to the next-door neighbours for schooling. This alternative venue school had a big office and a separate desk. He was not allowed to speak or interrupt the adults in the room so quietly got on with his work. It turns out he didn't do this at all. He returned home from his first school day at the neighbours with very little accomplished, even with the seventeen-year-old from the same school assisting him where he could. Being at work for these two days, there was little I could do to support. On day three, my own work was closed down and I was forced to furlough as per the government guidelines. This meant I could take on the role of full-time teacher for Lucas.

My teaching style is varied – from stern, to frustrated, to dumbfounded, to caring, to high fives. Not your average teacher, and it turns out that, even with a lot of class room experience teaching army cadets, I'm not that good doing it full time. I was a natural at maths, still using all the basic skills today in business. English was another of my A-levels, which I really enjoyed. Therefore I was quite happy to teach improper fractions and metaphorical poems in the same day. What I wasn't prepared for was Lucas' complete and utter lack of an attention span and his numerical dyslexia. Which it turns out he's happy to switch on and off at a whim. I'm not the only one, I know that. During the COVID-19 pandemic, every family household in the country had to make the same change to their lives. It was also very interesting to work closely with Lucas on his school work. I was learning what makes him tick more. I've found out that he's very creative and very practical. If you just throw numbers at him, he shuts down. If you throw discounted percentages of a new pair of trainers and tell him he only has to pay half of it, he gets it straight away.

When we introduced him to his new school, we insisted on him getting a teacher's assistant full time to work with him. Without having that additional support in a remote environment, it was up to me to learn that part of his support network and adapt the role over time. I found it confusing that, in just one example of a subject, I had been able to identify his strengths and weaknesses in a relatively short period of time. The school, however, had never let us know these shortfalls. Our parents-teacher meetings were all singing praises for his enthusiasm and focus. It just goes to prove that the issues in the schooling system, when put to the test with the kimono fully open to bare all, there are systematic failings in the process and the reporting. It does make me wonder whether virtual schooling is actually the better of the two options and should be made available in the future. Perhaps some of the more proactive parents will opt in. The amount of outdoor education, baking, supervising intellectual YouTube, and seeking informative activities has greatly improved due to lockdown. We are certainly a closer unit because of it, and it demonstrated an increase in our dedication to each other as a family unit than we have ever done before.

In addition to school, we had to manage lunch, playtime, and after-school activities. These often included helping us with our own activities to reduce anxieties and worries of the outside world. Gardening, painting, home improvement, deep cleaning, and car cleaning to name just a few. We also had the luxury of living on the Kent Downs area, so the walks from our front door were varied, extensive, and out of the public eye. We would often meet with the neighbours on the walk and off load each other's problems in order to retain some sort of sanity. No worries in our mind if we kept social distance and were careful of what we did outside the home. Washing hands, staying two metres apart and shopping once a week for essentials only.

I fear for the families that really couldn't do it and ended up breaking apart. In a normal world, there is child abuse on a worrying scale. If you put that into a situation where parents and children are tested to their limits, I worried daily about the impact on social services. I appreciate there is nothing we can do more than we are, we are at our limit at this stage in our career. We were managing a highly demanding child, but I did wonder, through the days of Lockdown 1.0, if I could do more. I wondered if they would relax restrictions and open more homes if they could to children in need. My nature is to help and support people, so I volunteered and also got a job as a porter in the Nightingale Hospital, which was never used. Perhaps the thought of helping others served only to confirm my desire to increase our brood, whether it be for short, medium, or long term placements.

The second time the government announced a three-week lockdown, we were possibly at the stage where we would be ready to start moving around again, but we had also settled into a routine. School was going well, and evening activities were planned, with a binge of Harry Potter for the evenings. The garden had never looked better, the weather was helping immensely, being the warmest on record. I was the director of an amusement park at the time and couldn't help but wonder about the other records I had planned to break at work, which the weather certainly would have helped achieve. No need to dwell, but it would have been nice, and I know Lucas loved coming to see me at work. Of course he did, his foster dad was the boss of an amusement park. What more could a child ask for.

We had worked out there is, however, one way to increase our brood without the need for a supervising social worker to cross-examine our entire life and critique what we do at every turn. My fortieth birthday was celebrated in lockdown and my present was probably the best thing anyone could be gifted. A white German shepherd puppy, who we named Artemus. Artemus, the male spelling of Artemis The Greek Goddess of the Hunt, got his name after his dad, who was named Zeus. When I went to pick him up, he took one look at me, then immediately sunk into the crook of my arm and fell asleep. He was the most chilled out and relaxed puppy you could ever ask for. That didn't mean, however, that the challenges of a new puppy were gone. I still needed to stay up all night for two weeks and nurse his separation anxiety. He still ate his way through most of the skirting boards in the house, and if there was a trainer within biting distance, he'd have it. He was, however, the very best of therapy for us all and took up all our time and more.

This second lockdown week did not include Easter, not that it made a difference, every day was blending into the next anyway. It was becoming too easy to relax in our newly tidied garden with a barbecue at four p.m. as it felt like it was the summer holidays already. The realisation that we may not get an official summer holiday at all, especially not a foreign one, was becoming all too real. We started to create the perfect lockdown staycation. I could lead a wine and cheese tasting for the adults. I have a plethora of team building games and fun activities that I could plan. The Kent Downs walk would be great as a group. Camping in the garden, barbecues, and limbo competitions. We can make this work if we put a little imagination into it. Hoping that a few activities in the area would be open by August meant that the kids could enjoy high ropes, paint ball, and horse riding.

I was made redundant from the theme park, totally expected given the circumstances, and the COVID-19 drama was proving to be bigger than anyone expected. Not one to sit still too long, I managed to start a new business running a hotel in a nearby village. We opened briefly in the summer before Lockdown 2.0. During that time, Lucas really came out of his shell. We had struggled for over a year to find Lucas' strengths in life. He wasn't naturally academic or sporty. He would try and turn to the arts, but his best efforts were damned by his lack of attention and patience. At the hotel, however, he was keen as mustard to help out. He would welcome guests, skip around the restaurant, and act in a very professional manner to all including the staff. Making chef's cups of tea in the morning to helping out the housekeeping team. He was a natural in hospitality and his work ethic was impressive. Didn't matter how much I tried to get him to sit down and relax, he would find something else to help out with. It really was a pleasure to see him come out of his shell. We asked him how he would like to be introduced to people as quite likely being the local hotelier in the village, lots of people will want to know all about us. As a sign of his acceptance of his permanent placement, he was quite happy to be referred to as our foster son and had no problem telling people that his foster dads own a hotel. Straight Dad and Gay Dad, of course.

Between lockdown 2.0 and 3.0, it became clear that the problems of before, which were specialised and unique in their presentation to us, were quickly being replaced with the same problems all parents face. I assure you that the title of professional parent does not give you super powers in being any better at home-schooling than anyone else. The mental strain on all children that have had to give up a year of their childhood to COVID-19 is not just suffered by children in care. If anything, being a looked after child made Lucas more resilient to the effects of the lockdowns. It was, for us, a shared level of pain that the whole country felt together and shared that pain online, on social posts, and in the media. Instead of being alone and suffering, we all suffered together. We all hated home schooling, but we loved being with each other and spending more time together. Bonding like we would never have been able to do without it. We had a lot more time for each other. If it wasn't for us having to play school teacher during the day or having to exhaust our own ability to entertain him without leaving the house, it would have been perfect. Incidentally, he quickly caught up on the education part, too. No longer was he classified as being two years behind his year group. He was actually on track.

Our second annual review came round as quickly as the first one. Lo and behold, it was done remotely due to COVID-19 lockdown rules. I certainly didn't believe that, after the first one was cancelled, the second would also be held remotely. This time round, we weren't even required to be in the meeting at all. We were called to inform us that our panel had been successful. It gets less exciting every time you're told but we were showered with praise for the work we had done with Lucas already. The conversation of having more kids came up. We wanted to be considered for three children placements. We wanted to increase our brood, no matter how temporary. We wanted to share our successes with Lucas with other children. We were addicted.

15

5 August 2021 – Second Placement

From day one, Robin and I wanted to have a big family. I am from a sibling group of three and Robin had six from his mother's side and another two half siblings from his father's side. When we made the decision to foster, as opposed to adopt or surrogate, we made the conscious decision that the more the merrier. If they were on respite care, emergency care, short term or long term, we would have an open-door policy for children in our care. We imagined big family holidays; caravanning, camping, or the more glamours villas or ski lodges full of mess, noise, and group chaos. Our house, we pictured, was full of different aged, different sized and probably different coloured kids all challenging us in different ways. Robin was always more reserved than me and the voice of reason to be able to weigh in with the logistical challenges of running a business alongside being professional parents; and now he was developing an unhealthy cleaning habit, in my mind, as the thought of children rubbing jam into his Laura Ashley sofa suite brought him out in a shiver.

The conversation of a second child has been a hot topic lately and if we ever run out of 'normal' conversation – weather, school, food, or weekend – we turn to the topic of a 'second child'. There is much debate between myself and Robin. I am rather relaxed about the whole thing – he is rather particular. He wants a seven-year-old girl. It's not difficult to see why – he wants the process of primary school and the fun that goes with finger painting. He wants to be able to discuss the finer details of bringing up a little girl with friends – I also feel his feminine side will be better challenged with a girl than a boy. I very much enjoy martial arts, rugby, snowball fights, and those chats about girls. I enjoy it because I draw on personal experience to deal with it and take pride in being able to advise accordingly. Robin, however, doesn't have as many of those masculine experiences to draw on. I think that, with a girl, he will enjoy sharing his experience of hair styling, shopping, talking about boys, and the challenges all that brings. He will try and mention to Lucas about how Brad Pitt is good looking, and all Lucas can do is spit out whatever he is shovelling into his mouth and burst out 'disgusting' or something similar. A little girl also brings with it new challenges that Robin and I haven't been exposed to yet, so there is a view on how that challenges us as carers rather than people.

That dream appears to be more difficult to actually execute than it is to discuss and talk about. It's no apparent fault of any one person or body. I was recently in a COVID-safe safeguarding meeting and a foster parent on there had a sibling group of four. That sounded more like our kind of chaos to me, and I couldn't help but feel a little jealous. The initial thought of that environment being right up my street was quickly followed by some words of sense from Robin rattling around in the back of my mind. Had we not been as focused as we were with Lucas, I don't believe we would ever had had as much of an impact on his improvement as we have. That improvement of Lucas, from when he first moved in to now, is massive. Although not all our credit, we share that responsibility with his school and our nominated carers around him. I do believe, however, that we could have helped one long term or several emergency placements along the way given the chance without negatively impacting on Lucas.

When we were first appointed as approved carers from our panel, we had the authority to be placed with up to two children from zero to eighteen years old. We were told that this number can be reviewed in line with the progress we made but, as newbies to the world of fostering, they were being cautious. We were happy with this but, after Lucas was placed with a bed blocking that has gone on for over two years, we've never had a chance to increase our responsibility.

We met William on 9 August 2021. He was seven years old and had moved four times just this summer. He suffered from PTSD, just like Lucas, and shared many of the behavioural traits we had experienced when Lucas first moved in with us. William, however, was four years younger than Lucas was when he moved in with us. This gives us confidence that we can catch his bad behaviour nice and early, giving us an opportunity to influence his life a little earlier, and giving him the best chance of a normal life as soon as possible. The similarity in behaviour issues reminded us of Lucas, so we were happy to help him. Other carers would have run a mile if you read his back story, but the kind of issues experienced were just what we specialised in.

We went to see him in his current placement, twenty-five minutes from our house, as a bit of an intro and warm up. He had been told he was moving again and was not taking it very well. He was not happy about another move, so we took Lucas with us for support, and he was brilliant. He played with him on the computer, and they talked about what they like to do. He relaxed a little and we got to discuss his needs with his current carer. We found out that he just likes to play on his computer all day, his behaviour is poor, tantrums, self-harm, and inappropriate behaviour. There may also have been sexual abuse at some point in his life as some of the things he says are of a sexualised nature. Nothing we haven't seen before. Often people forget that, in the care system, we'd had one of the most difficult children on the planet in Richard. There is no child worse than that kid, so we're relatively relaxed when other carers tell us horror stories.

Three days later, he arrived at the house with his carer in tow, and a social worker supervising the transition, like we needed a chaperone. He was very nervous and generally unhappy about leaving his current carer. We made a promise that we would see him on the weekend and go out for lunch. This made him feel a bit better, so he could say see you later as opposed to goodbye, which he was dead against. Some kids have trigger words that can bring back unhappy memories. We think goodbye may be one of those trigger words because it's associated with all the negative things in his life. As soon as we got him through the door, and he had met Artemus the therapy dog, the tears turned to smiles and all was well with the world. We made beige food as a treat. The beige food I refer to as all that naughty food kids like. Apparently he only ate beige food. When we discussed the need to eat broccoli or he's not going to be able to play on his computer, we soon got him eating vegetables. Perhaps people hadn't tried hard enough. We did not tolerate the tantrums. Instead of giving in, we just increase the punishment until we find the limits on both parties. He was settling in well, minding his 'thank you's', and generally improving rapidly on a daily basis. As with Lucas, we did not experience the behaviour described in his report. The aggression and the emotional breakdowns just didn't manifest. We picked up the bedtime routine pretty quickly and his manners became impeccable, even picking Lucas up for his slight indiscretions.

We started to believe in our strategy more as we saw William improve on a daily basis. We started to believe we may actually have a secret recipe that although may only work with kids with PTSD or young boys with attachments issues, we were confident that the successes with Lucas could actually be repeated with William. Us and our support group were just what he needed. The support group we now referred to as the 'Royal Borough' because our neighbour had earned herself an MBE. It was the magical combination of friendly, approachable, CRB-checked neighbours and us that, combined, made us unflappable and unbeatable. We were going to do it again. And probably again until we were old and wrinkly.

16

20 August 2021 – Our Life Sentence

Our time with William was short-lived.

It was Friday, 20 August at five-thirty p.m. when we got the call from our Supervising Social Worker.

Robin picked up the phone.

"Hi Robin, it's Noah [our social worker]. We're coming to pick up the boys and remove them out of your care based on safeguarding issues. We will be with you in one hour."

Robin couldn't believe it and came up to the bedroom to wake me up from a nap to hand me the phone. I had been with the Army Cadets on our annual training camp for the past two weeks, which was a pretty exhausting affair considering I was also head cheffing in my hotel in the evenings as we were short staffed. I had also picked up my long service medal in a very humbling ceremony, with speeches, photographs, and a march past salute. It was all very impressive for little William, who took it upon himself to shout out his pride in the otherwise silent audience.

I asked Noah to repeat and explain himself.

"What on earth do you mean a safeguarding issue?"

I was getting a little upset. He didn't explain himself, of course. We only knew that he would be here in an hour, and we were to pack a small bag for each of the boys and get them ready to be removed from our care. We were racking our brains for what it could be, I immediately blamed Robin, as he hadn't got the new bathroom finished in time for William's arrival while we were on holiday. I thought that having two bathrooms not three was the reason. Stupidly, I then decided that I would tile the bathroom myself and fit the bath, so the boys didn't have to shower in our ensuite. A momentary lack of clarity, which Robin put right straight away, as he always does.

Noah arrived at seven p.m., ninety minutes after calling us and informed us that two separate emergency carers were on their way to pick up the boys. Not only were they leaving but to separate homes. This caused a bit of a backlash from the boys to say the least. William and Lucas decided they were going to put up a fight.

"They can't physically take us if we just refuse to go, can they?"

Lucas was the slightly calmer of the two.

"I won't go, I'll hit them with my lightsabre if I have to."

William was slightly more hysteric, similar to my own current emotional state. I know I'm supposed to be a professional parent and the calm one around emergency situations, but the complete lack of information and the careless attitude of everyone 'not saying anything' put me, Robin, and the boys in a very, very difficult situation. None of us wanted what was happening to happen, so none of us really wanted to comply. Armed with lightsabres and nerf guns, the boys weren't going anywhere with anyone.

Two hours later, Noah got a call from his supervisor. So the Supervising Social Worker's Supervisor. Bureaucracy at its finest. She explained to me that it was not the bathroom – phew, missed a curve ball there having to live with my tiling efforts for the rest of our lives. There was a situation that they cannot divulge that will need to be investigated, but the priority is to remove the boys from our care and that has to happen tonight. At this point, we had Noah and two emergency carers standing outside our front door. Three men, all intent on disrupting the boys' lives for apparent good reason. However, this was, we all felt, an aggressive show of force that started to antagonise and cause trauma for both us and the boys. It created such a drama that this commotion had the interest of our neighbours by now, who as we know are the loveliest and kindest neighbours anyone could hope to live next door to. They are also our nominated emergency carers should anything ever happen. Well, something was happening. They immediately offered to step in and care for the boys. We discussed, under pressure, that if the problem was us, we would relinquish care of the boys to them for the short term. They could move into our house and cause as little disruption to the boys as possible while we moved into the hotel. This, however, was not as easy as we thought. The reasons for us not being able to care for them were unclear, so we were spit balling. Perhaps we could swap houses, rather than move into the hotel. This was not possible as apparently we would be too close. The initial thought of moving into the hotel and leaving the boys at home also needed senior authorisation. We thought that this situation would blow over in a week or two. Then we can calm down, sort out whatever was going on, and all get back to normal in the next few days.

William's social carer immediately preferred that idea as he was considered a relatively high-risk placement anyway and being cared for by someone he knows is a much better idea. He had nowhere to go, had run out of options anyway, and being a high-risk placement, not many were qualified to deal with his emotional challenges. Lucas' out of hours contact, however, had a different approach.

"Remove him from the house now – if you can't do it, call the police and have them remove him."

When I heard this advice passed on by Noah, I now started to feel just a little anxious about the whole situation. The threat to have the boys removed by the police was a frightening thought and my natural 'Super Dad' defence reaction was 'just try it'. I quickly realised that these boys had had this kind of situation happen to them already in their lives. They had, at some point, been removed from their biological parents and I would understand if this felt similar in nature to them. I certainly wasn't going to leave them with a lasting memory of that nature involving me, so I needed to end this as positively as I could. The relapse in their journey of therapeutic repair to their mental health was exactly the kind of thing we protected them from. My momentary lapse of faith in the system, and my instincts to just stand there, was replaced with some sense. I had an honest chat with Lucas and convinced him that he needs to be the bigger of the two brothers and go with the nice foster carer who really just wants to help out. With an outpour of love and affection, tears and hugs, he reluctantly promised to go. Only if I fed him one more time. I had a nice stew in the Aga, so it was a bit of a farewell dinner before he left. Nerf guns unloaded and racked, he sighed, grabbed his prepared overnight bag, and headed for the door. As he walked to the car, shoulders as low hung as they could be, with the hood of his snuggle jumper firmly over ninety per cent of his head, he looked back, spun on his heels, and ran back into my arms. Just one last hug, just in case. I'd forgotten that he's been through all of this before – he knew what he needed to do. All of the one last hugs that he had regretted not giving in the past were all now channelling through me.

"I love you so much – I love you both so, so much," he whispered, with Noah close enough so he could hear clearly the personal in nature chat and log it in his report.

Lucas left us.

William, lucky boy, got to stay in his own bed. Put there by our neighbours, who dutifully and affectionately tucked him in.

The next day, Lucas' district changed their minds. Knowing full well the fragility of Lucas' mental health and how vulnerable he must be feeling, they agreed to let him go back to his home and be looked after by our neighbours until we can sort out this nightmare, whatever it was. His own social worker had been in court all day, so she hadn't been made aware, and when told of the rather hurried way it was executed she was seriously unimpressed with the handling of the situation. She knew us well and knew the accusation was malicious. She had our backs and immediately insisted Lucas was taken home. Without much sleep, and still emotional, he returned and ran to the comfort of the dog's furry mane. We had returned the dog to the house after taking him with us to the hotel, knowing full well that his job as child therapy dog was more important than adult therapy dog. The therapy dog that I so desperately needed right now was needed more by the vulnerable kids in our care. The therapy dog was suffering greatly, too, from the shake up and emotion of the past twenty-four hours. He couldn't understand why Robin and I were so upset or why we were travelling in the middle of night without the boys. A German Shepherd is incredibly sensitive to emotion and you could feel that he, too, was feeling vulnerable in this whole situation.

It wasn't until a week later that the police showed up at the hotel to confirm what was going on. A whole week of not being able to talk to the boys or go to our own home. Still nothing had been confirmed about exactly what was happening. We did, however, hear through the grapevine that Richard had been arrested by the police and, during the arrest, he had blamed us for the way he was acting. He had blamed his gay uncles for his behaviour, and I guess we're easy targets, so it didn't take long for the authorities to put two and two together and make five. It's funny how the world is inherently homophobic towards gay couples sometimes. We have had to deal with being called perverts and paedos our whole lives. The new version 'nonce' is also bantered around. This whole journey of becoming parents, although well intentioned, had been intermittently splattered with homophobia at every turn. The initial interviews in 2008, the attack on us in the bar in 2018, and now. Lambasted and tarnished with the social views that gay men are sexually deviant or promiscuous, and the horrors of the 1950s incarnations, haunt us all still. A straight couple, I believe, would never been as suspected as we were or interrogated with such venom as we were. You would, and should, dismiss this as a malicious allegation of jealousy and greed within days. As a gay couple, we have had to build up a high level of resilience to homophobia. Never did we think that an accusation of that nature would ever affect us as greatly as it has. I remember being the victim of a homophobic attacked on Robin's birthday in November 2003. We were jumped on by four lads who didn't like us holding on to each other's hands. They came off much worse, and when the police finally arrived, all four were on the floor nursing relative injuries. We got arrested for it. Goes to show how the police work. The next morning, we were released with no charge. Not an apology or an attempt to press charges for homophobia. Perhaps it would have been easier to let them beat us up and then we may have actually been considered victims. At that point, I thought perhaps that the situation in 2003 was our one and only homophobic attack. This couldn't possibly still be happening in 2021, could it? Being let off after spending the night in the cells was a sobering experience we hoped never to repeat. It wasn't until much later that homophobia was made a hate crime, so we had absolutely no leg to stand on at the time. We also felt a tinge of homophobia from the police that night, too, as if we were 'asking for it' by holding hands. A traumatising event for us with no support offered or available.

It affects us greatly today more than ever because, in our current situation, it is not actually us that is the most hurt by all this. The emotional pain and hurt inflicted on the two boys in our care is unfortunately going to haunt them and stick with them forever. If I were them, I would never trust another adult again. During the past two and a half years, we would tell Lucas daily that this was his forever home. An overwhelming feeling that we had lied now built up in our stomachs. We felt like liars, we felt so many emotions – none of them happiness or joy. We felt guilt, fear, anger, and a level of sadness never felt before, it was staggering. It was interesting to know that, when your mental health is tested as it is, it can actually get stronger not weaker. I had never felt so mentally strong as I did that week, just terribly, terribly sad.

The interview was interesting, the thirteen hours in custody wasn't. Although, never to look a gift horse in the mouth, I took the opportunity to do some learning and managed to pick up a book, National Geographic's 'The Golden Ratio: the mathematical language of beauty'. Wow, what a read. I recommend it to anyone if you happen to be locked up in a cell for thirteen hours. I obtained it with the notion that it may send me to sleep, but it did the opposite and kept me reading the entire book. The perfect ratio is basically all around us and follows a mathematically perfect ratio of 1.618, just in case you wanted to know. The Mona Lisa, the Acropolis, and even credit cards are all a consequence of the perfect ratio.

The interview was long-winded and asked many specific questions about our relationship with Richard. What kind of behaviour he demonstrated and why we thought he would make an accusation like this? It was very personal and, in explaining many of the actions of 2018, I realised that we had made mistakes. Those mistakes were our training for getting it right the next time. We had no training to handle Richard and no system of reporting either. It was a really difficult time for all three of us and, knowing what we know now, we would never have taken him in in the first place. I think perhaps he realised that and that may have been his motivation for blaming us. The details of the accusation were academic to me and to Robin, as he was blanketing us both equally, which reinforced our faith in each other. Robin and I were never stronger than at this moment, fighting something together as a team. Our relationship was not going to be beaten by Richard, or anyone for that matter. We worried about the boys mainly and wanted so desperately to be there for them and make all this go away. But now at least we understood why it was happening and realised that the actions everyone had taken were for the safety of the boys and the protection of them. We knew that now and could at least explain to them that it wasn't anything either of them had done. It was an 'us' problem and we were going to fix it – or at least try bloody hard to fix it. One thing, however, continued to play on my mind, and it was Richard's mental health. I feared he would do something even more stupid, like take his own life. He had tried it once before, and if he was feeling so low that he needed to do this to us, he would possibly be thinking of the one thing we had worked hard to steer him away from. Despite all the hatred he was acting out on us, I was still worried about him.

Lucas had his police interview. Being thirteen, he was considered old enough to be able to be interviewed and express his views – shortly afterwards, we were told that we would be able to have supervised visits with him. They must not have been concerned about us and him then. Every scenario played through my mind of us being relatively risky carers. An example would be that if I had worked late at the hotel one night, Lucas knew I'd need a cup of tea in the morning. He brought it to my bedside most mornings before heading to school. This broke so many rules as carers, but it also normalised our family existence. In effect, Lucas was in my bedroom, alone, with me in bed. An outsider learning this for the first time would understandably be concerned. To me, it's my foster son bringing me a cup of tea in bed before he goes to school because he wants to see me before he starts his day. In reflection on this and other perfectly innocent situations, we realised that our approach was going to have to change in the future. We would be more guarded and more cautious in everything we did.

The thought of seeing Lucas again was overwhelming, we were so happy.

"Are you sure you don't mind taking some time away from the hotel and meeting us?" Lucas' social worker was adamant that we needed to be considered in the decision-making process too.

"Are you mad, I'll close the hotel down if it means seeing Lucas again."

My response possibly helped cement any priorities I had in

life. We met up with Lucas and went shopping for back-to-school things. At each moment, his social worker said she would pick up the bills, but we politely declined. As far as we were concerned, we were still his parents and could still provide for him, regardless of if we were being reimbursed for it or not. We nipped into the bowling alley for a bit of ten pin before heading out to dinner. The bowling was so much fun and, gently, we had managed to coax out a few laughs and smiles from Lucas throughout the day. I was enjoying myself so much, I almost forgot what was happening, then it hit me like a train. Tears started to roll down my cheeks that I had to hide. We were having so much fun and I was so sad knowing what was at risk, the risk that these magical moments were going to be too few in the near future at least.

His social worker took me to one side, "For God's sake, Larry, pull yourself together."

She then took hold of her actions and apologised for being so crass. I assured her that's exactly the advice I needed. I did just that and pulled myself together. Lucas, bless him, took the time to remind me of something too.

"You haven't done this before, have you? Don't worry, I have, it will be okay," he said it in a caring, therapeutic manner I reserved usually for the way I spoke to him.

He was referring to experiences of family visits with his own biological family. It made me emotional again because he was obviously thinking of us as his real family, and it hurt to know how upset he was not to be with us.

The level of strength of character in this boy blew me away. What happened to the little boy who struggled to function as a normal child? He's now consoling me, an Army Reserves Captain, rugby player, and entrepreneur. He really is the strongest person I know. At dinner, we talked about how he needed to behave with his new carers. We supported his move and tried to give him as much of our strength as we could, what little we had. At dinner, he plated his food from the bowls of curry and rice placed on the table with the skill and care of a Michelin-starred chef. He seasoned it from a height and smiled at me with that grin as big as his face that I recognised from the first day I met him. I had taught him well, and he knew just how to pay me a compliment without saying anything at all.

At this stage, Lucas' social worker was the only person who was saying anything positive to us. She supported us and believed in us completely. Everyone else treated us, we felt, as guilty until proven innocent. Even if they weren't, it felt like it. We had all our electrical goods removed from our house for forensic examination, and that feeling of guilt was huge. I guess when it comes to children and the law, you are genuinely guilty until proven innocent rather than the other way round. We had been locked up, interviewed, ignored by our team of care workers, and everyone we met judged us. Even if they supported us publicly, you had a sinking feeling that everyone was talking about us and questioning what was going on. The amount of people who would say to us, 'If it's true, then obviously the boys will not be able to return to you.' That was the most hurtful. I'm not sure people said it to be hurtful, but it stung deep. 'If we were guilty' was damning and accusatory in itself. Robin lost contact with most of his family over the matter. This surprised us both and added gravity to an already heavy situation. Robin was so upset at the loss of his family, all but two of them sided with Richard. My family obviously knew both Richard and me well, and they didn't require any convincing. It would, however, have been lovely to get some support from people that knew us from our fostering agency. They all took a big step back and followed their policy as a matter of course. We were appointed a mentor who had been through something similar. She called us once before the police took our phones and she became estranged after that. Noah's supervisor was unknown to us and, as part of their policy, needed to be totally neutral to the situation. She became our social worker as Noah handed in his notice and left shortly after our incident. That didn't help one bit. We didn't need or want neutral; we wanted a friendly voice and a supportive approach. However, it just made us a feel more and more guilty as time went on. Noah gave very little support in the way of counsel. He, too, had to been told to be neutral. A day before his impending resignation date, he eventually became available. He turned up at the house for an unannounced visit, something that was normal should you actually have children in your care, only to be reminded that the boys had been taken away – by him! He didn't realise we were going to be there, thinking that our neighbours would still be in residence at the house, and we would be at the hotel. It was uncomfortable for everyone and although he was trying hard to avoid us, this unplanned meeting forced him to engage in an adult conversation with us about the ludicrous situation and how it had unfolded. There is no law that states if someone is accused of assault on a minor, everyone around them has to be neutral. What really needs to happen is that you should be offered support and convincing that this will all be over at some point, and we will look back and laugh, or cry. Then if you are wrong and the accused gets found guilty, then get over it. Ask yourself why you didn't see it sooner and move on. You did the right thing by supporting someone who needed it, whatever they've done. When you don't get through on the phone – call again, then again, and again until you do. Then when they answer the phone, ask if everything is okay and why the phone wasn't answered. We needed to be supported with enthusiasm and care. We needed that therapeutic care that we offered as adults to children offered to us. Working for a charity that specialised in that, we expected it to be on tap. It wasn't.

Four weeks after the incident, we were informed our bail was going to be delayed by another two months while awaiting investigations. During this time, we had researched all we could, we had hired a great lawyer, and we were prepared to fight whatever battles that laid ahead. Our biggest problem was the outcome, as we didn't know what it was going to be. An accusation of this level of seriousness could have a number of outcomes:

One. Substantiated – which means they have evidence the crime took place, which is impossible so that's not on our minds.
Two. False – the accusation is proved to be false, backed with evidence.
Three. Malicious – the accusation is found to be a malicious attack and with evidence to prove that.
Four. Unfounded – which means there is no evidence or a proper basis to support the allegation.
Five. Unsubstantiated – the accusation cannot be proved to be true or false therefore you are neither proved guilty or innocent.

We were dearly hoping for false or malicious but were not holding our breath as we very much doubted that, without a redaction statement from the accuser, either of those will happen.

If the accusation is unfounded, we might, just might, have a chance to get the boys back and rebuild our lives. If, however, the accusation is found to be unsubstantiated, we will never get the boys back and may be offered a plea deal, including time on the offenders list. If this happens, our lives as we know them will be over. Naturally, humans tend to worry about the worst. Every morning, I would wake up from this recurring nightmare that I will never be a dad again. I will never be able to help young people again, and never will I be able to influence or support the youth of today. We would need to take a complete change in direction of life. We would often spend the evenings planning out these life changes should they be required. One was to buy a boat and sail to the Caribbean to take up a life as a pirate. Another was to buy two houseboats in Amsterdam, rent one out on Airbnb, and live in the other. Sometimes renting both out whilst travelling around the world. What really saddened us was that we wouldn't be doing what we really loved which was looking after young people and making them get the best futures they could ask for. Our initial mission was that, if we couldn't procreate to add our genes to the future of the human race, we would influence those young people who needed it.

The days passed and turned into weeks. We were granted regular supervised contact with Lucas as part of managing his own mental strength. This was labelled 'family time', as it would if we were his biological parents and he had been put into care. I guess the idea was that we were considered his family and the importance of our contact was reassuring. He fluctuated from one in ten to three in ten on his emotional happiness scale. Sometimes, if we were lucky, he'd jump up to six in ten when with us. We took the dog for walks on the beach, went out for lunch, and had long chats about school, life, and sometimes

Richard. He was confused and hurting, unsure why the police weren't taking his word over Richard's. All he wanted was to be home and his want to return home wasn't enough to persuade the police of our innocence no matter how much we wanted it to. On one such visit, we decided to meet at the hotel. A special place in our family as we had spent lockdown Christmas there and the staff were also like an extension of his family. He beamed at the thought of coming. His arrival showed that beam was still in place from a week before. He crept into the kitchen and leaned against the wall, watching me work a busy Sunday lunch shift. It took maybe forty-five seconds for me to notice him before I leapt over the pass to get my weekly squeeze. No regard for the pile of tickets that was getting longer and longer in the heat of a busy Sunday lunch. He has always enjoyed surprising me and takes great pleasure when successful. I realised I had let my guard down over the last three months. When living with this little ninja, I would always be prepared with the awareness of a mountain lion as to the potential of an attack being right round the corner. I would need to work on this should Lucas come back to live with us.

During these weeks, I had taken the time to research more about false accusations and I came across a paper called, 'The Impact of Being Wrongly Accused of Abuse in Occupations of Trust: Victims' Voices' by Carolyn Hoyle, Naomi-Ellen Speechley, and Ros Burnett (University of Oxford Centre for Criminology). It was an incredibly interesting read and wish I had found it sooner. Some of the information I obtained that I found particularly interesting I have quoted in this chapter. I also found FACT – a charity supporting falsely accused carers and teachers. This website also has a link to the report, so it's an easy one-stop-shop for people who are going through a false allegation.

We are certain of the false and malicious accusation. However, we feel guilty in sense of feeling only. Guilty for not protecting ourselves, or for letting Richard think this was his only way out. As discussed in our interviews with the police, his accusation is not the first time and, on previous occasions, he had the emotional support of his parents to discuss it clearly and to understand that it was malicious. This time, however, the greed and rising popularity associated with seeking compensation is greater than the sensible and adult approach to the wild and damaging accusation.

Webster, R. (2005) *The Secret of Bryn Estyn: The Making of a Modern Witch Hunt* wrote:

What is not generally understood is that the act of making a false allegation of abuse can and often does bring a feeling of psychological satisfaction... People who have previously felt overlooked and insignificant may suddenly find themselves the centre of attention, concern and sympathy. At the same time the idea that they are now engaged in a battle against evil, in which many other people, including counsellors and social workers, are fighting alongside them, can be a source of great emotional energy. It may give people both a raison d'être and a feeling of strength and solidarity which they did not previously have. (Webster, 2005, p.131-2)

We are also convinced that possibly another stimulus to complain might be the suggestions he made to us that he may have repressed memories of abuse from a previous adult charged with his care, and that such abuse could be the cause of his current difficulties in behaviour, substance abuse, and offending – of which all are rife. The long-term traumatic effects of childhood abuse are long-reaching consequences on self-esteem, self-regulation, and the ability to process or manifest those memories into current day situations. Childhood abuse more often does not include sexual abuse and can build over time down to emotional neglect, detachment from biological parents, or an unstable and erratic home. Being able to explain and justify personal behavioural difficulties and mental health problems as the outcomes of abuse is likely to be a powerful motivator for an individual to believe that they were abused. Richard has, in the past, stolen from us, assaulted us, and threatened to make allegations of this type of thing. Each time, we forgave him and used it as a learning platform to try and change his behaviour. To an outsider, perhaps this approach does seem a little too generous, but that's what we do.

The recent reporting of high-profile sex offenders in the media, like Epstein, Savile, and Glitter, followed by the public revulsion towards child abuse, has led to a culture of hyper-vigilance about these types of offences. While this obviously helps in protecting vulnerable groups, it has also encouraged a suspicious, smoke-without-fire society. Therefore creating a group of people, the accused, a group of guilty people. The paper from Oxford university went on to explain:

'Confirmation bias' is the tendency to bolster a hypothesis by seeking consistent evidence while disregarding inconsistent information (Nickerson, 1998). In criminal investigations, a preference for hypothesis-consistent information undermines accuracy by leading investigators to overlook potentially relevant evidence that challenges their theory (O Brien and Ellsworth, 2006, p.5).

Changes in the approach to complaints about abuse were reflected in the new Guidelines on Prosecuting Cases of Child

Sexual Abuse, introduced in 2013. These steered prosecutors away from questioning the credibility of the complainant by challenging the myths' surrounding the reporting of sexual crimes (Crown Prosecution Service, 2013, para. 41). The Guidelines also specified that prosecutors should guard against looking for corroboration" of the victim s account' (para. 55)

A report in 2014 by Her Majesty s Inspector of Constabulary, 'Crime Recording: Making the Victim Count', recommended: The presumption that the victim should always be believed should be institutionalised while the practice of some forces of investigating first and recording later should be abandoned immediately (HMIC, 2014, para. 7.16). Following on from this, the Crown Prosecution Service and Metropolitan Police Service (2015) Action Plan on Rape asserts that prosecutors must focus their case on the behaviour of the accused, not the complainant' (p.2). Which is exactly what we are asking for. While such policies reassure victims that they will be believed and treated sympathetically, unfortunately they also pave the way for vexatious and erroneous claims to be believed.

All of this, and the other sixty-five pages of information went a long way to helping us understand the 'why's' behind the lengthy investigation and the processes that the police needed to follow.

Perhaps Jensen and Jensen summarised best how we are feeling at the moment and just the thought of being accused of such an awful crime will change us forever.

Hundreds more have been caught up in widespread police investigations and as a result have lost their professional reputation and personal standing. Lives have been shattered, careers have been lost and families have been torn apart.'
(Jensen and Jensen, 2011, p.iii)

So, we decided to just wait it out, as was the advice from everyone who didn't have to live the nightmare.

"Be patient and wait it out before you decide anything."

Sound advice should you not be worrying sick about whether you would be sent to prison for child sex offences. Obviously not going to happen, but the scenario played out in our heads regularly. You won't be able to convince me prison is only full of guilty people.

17

30 October 2021 – Conclusions

Twelve-thirty, in the middle of Saturday lunch service, I got a phone call from Robin. He was out picking up some change for the tills at the hotel. He sounded emotional and obviously the worst things were racing through my mind. He had got a call from the police. He didn't know what to say and stuttered his way through the next few sentences.

"No further action, they're not pursuing the investigation."

His emotion was happiness, something we hadn't felt in a long time. I physically felt the weight of the past ten weeks lift off my shoulders. The elation caused some tears and I started to hug everyone around me. My manager of the hotel, who had been sharing the emotions with me over the past two and half months, was also crying. We always hoped the outcome was going to be not guilty, because we weren't. However, the mind plays on the worst-case scenario and my daily nightmare was now over.

We couldn't tell Lucas yet as the future was still not known to anyone for sure. We had another face-to-face visit the next day and had already planned a shopping trip. My excitement was too much, and we decided to treat him as best we knew. We arranged for a personal shopper at a local designer outlet and decked him out in some new threads. We did a few catwalks, much to the enjoyment of the shop staff, and headed out for dinner. He reminded us that our bail date was coming up and was excited about the prospect of us knowing our fate. It was so tempting to tell him the investigation was over and there was no case to pursue. We still hadn't had it in writing and were advised not to tell anyone, but that advice fell on deaf ears, and we had told pretty much everyone. Our relationships with social workers, charities, and other professionals was so intertwined and because of such a closeness, we couldn't keep them all in the dark. We felt that they should know as soon as we did.

The physical weight on my shoulders of the whole ordeal was lifted and I walked a little taller because it. I was smiling, something I hadn't done very much in the past ten weeks. It felt strange and the emotion of happiness felt unusual to me, too. I can now understand why so many people can suffer debilitating anxiety or depression because of a situation like this. I can now empathise with other people who have been put through this. It has been awful, but now it's over and we wanted to celebrate it as much as possible. My thoughts moved to Richard as I'm sure he's not celebrating. He may be blaming us still. He may be prepared to retract his statement, or he may be wanting to appeal. I have no idea, but I thought of him and wished him well in my prayers.

Four days later, we got another phone call from our favourite participant in our wild, hectic journey, 'the supervisor'. She was her usual detached and unsympathetic self. She relayed to us word for word the response from the police to our probe for more information and a decision on our child care future in order for us to get Lucas back. The response from the police was this:

'I had asked Robin and Larry not to share this information until the paperwork is generated and forwarded to them.

However, I understand their wish for people to know quickly. The decision that there will be no further action taken against them has been taken due to there being insufficient evidence at this stage to proceed. I am unable to provide a detailed explanation to you other than to say that, in order to proceed further, we would need to be satisfied that there is sufficient evidence available to give a realistic prospect of conviction. The standard of proof in a criminal court is that of beyond all reasonable doubt, which is, of course, very high. In this case, the evidence that has been gathered during the course of the investigation has been reviewed and we do not believe that realistically we would have sufficient evidence to make a Jury sure.'

The local authority had this to say on the matter: "As this was closed due to insufficient evidence, my recommendation would be for a standards of care to look at the balance of probability. The way this is worded by the police leaves lots of questions. I will ask for more clarity upon this being formally signed off. Robin and Larry need to understand that the police have an outcome, but a safeguarding outcome is yet to come and may not be the same as [sic] police."

Our rollercoaster journey was not over yet and it looked like the sensible, evidence-based approach of the police was about to be handed to the opinions of the child health care system, which was, as we know so far in our life-long dealing with, unpredictable at best. We were now at the mercy of the system we have so dearly tried to support and so bitterly never really understood why it continued to fail the young people in our life.

I wish I could tell you everything was going to be okay. We don't even know where the future will take us – it's just so uncertain now. With this accusation hanging over us, we're not sure if we will ever be able to foster again. I'm not even sure if we want to at this stage. We have been so damaged mentally and our anxiety has been driven to its limits. I worry dreadfully for the future of the boys mostly. I also often think of Richard and how he must be feeling to make such a terrible accusation. Why he thought this was his only option. To literally ruin the lives of four people to save his own skin. Possibly in search of money, or just to be recognised by his own family. Recognition that he has always craved and never got, even with us coaching his mother and him on how we believed their relationship needs to develop.

On reflection of fostering in general, we found many looked after children do not resonate with their carers and flit from one home to another. Lucas had been to ten families, number eleven counting his current residence. Who knows how many more he will go to if he doesn't return to us. William had changed hands four times just the summer before he arrived with us. Their own issues with attachment or possible abuse, either on their part or on the part of their birth parents, is a recipe for failure in general. With Lucas, we managed to luck out, or was it a result of hard work? Until William, we thought it may be luck, but he proved we may actually be good at this as he improved greatly on a daily basis. Will Lucas be our one and only success story? Is it too short a moment to even call it a success story? There are so many questions and perhaps I'll write a reprint in five years' time. A pipe dream at best in my current situation. I do so hope that is possible and I hope we find the resilience within us to carry on looking after the most demanding of young people to support them in their life. I'm sure I'll know a lot more if we do, but I'm also sure there will be a lot of unanswered questions still.

When it comes to me, I used to believe that I couldn't be more happy to consider any referral for any child. I am of the mind that we get whatever we get. We open the gates of the house and take the first child in the queue. Metaphorically, of course. I was particularly keen on an unaccompanied minor – another care term for asylum-seeking minors without any adult representation. I think that they are one of the most at-risk groups in the world that really could benefit from a positive living environment. Of course, I've considered the impact on religion, particularly Muslim, and how gay dads may be a real challenge for young Muslims. But really, it's up to them. If a young Muslim asylum seeker is happy having two gay dads, then who am I to stop them. Until now, however, that was always a possibility, but the accusation from Richard has damaged my enthusiasm and putting myself at risk is really an awful experience that I never want to repeat. I used to drop hints to Robin that I'm open to anything, 'even an asylum seeker', hoping it will spark a passionate conversation about the ethics or matching with Lucas and William but so far it has fallen on deaf ears. Either deaf ears or carefree ears. His desire for an eight-year-old girl is still pretty strong.

The other group of at-risk people is parent and child, often referred to as mother and child. Although it wasn't my idea, I'm more and more keen as time goes on. I'm particularly good with young adults and Robin is particularly good with babies. I think, as a team, we would be formidable for the most challenging of parent-child combinations. We've had the training and are well aware of the challenging environment, but the only thing holding us back would be our social workers having complete confidence in our ability as carers. Any new incumbents will take time and energy, not easy when we're on our fourth social worker in two years. Another challenge for young people is the seemingly transient occupation that is social care. They either burn out, don't get paid enough, or get promotions. Any way you look at it, young people in care rarely have a consistent adult role model in their lives after going into 'the system'. It's no wonder that some statistics quote that seventy per cent of looked after children end up in the criminal justice system in some shape or form.

I was also keen on teenagers, a really difficult group of young people that many carers refuse to consider. It's such a shame as, although they come with a lot of baggage, mental challenges, and growing issues, they are also so much fun. To help them on the journey of becoming the very best young adults they can be is so rewarding. I have spent twelve years helping youngsters in the army cadet force and the rewards are so incredible. I've seen teenagers overcome ticks, speech impediments, confidence issues, depression, and anxiety. Not to mention acne, growing pains, sexual confusion, and anger issues. I've seen so much, albeit on a part-time basis, and I really want to challenge myself with a full-time commitment. I think that too many teenagers in care end up in group homes and there is really not much promise for them. Robin volunteers for the Young Life Foundation – our UK equivalent of Big Brother in the US. His current young person is sixteen and was moved to a group home for challenging behaviour. It appears to us that he has gained nothing from being there, apart from an increased desire to spend more time with Robin. I don't work in a home, but I can imagine there is very little personable care, including a good tucking in at night, or hugging after a challenging or emotional day. Something that Lucas has already reminded us of that he doesn't currently get.

"It's been three months since someone hugged me before bed." He would complain on his bi-weekly contacts with us.

I'm not aware but I'm sure group homes follow the rules

more than we do about professional care. I know Lucas particularly likes at least two big squeezes before bed. I can't imagine an orderly being as kind. Not that they're not kind. From reading referrals in the early days, I'm acutely aware that actually we shouldn't pigeonhole anyone, stereotype, or set strict requirements. We certainly didn't think a twelve-year-old boy on permanent placement was a good idea. We were pleasantly and happily wrong. Lucas made our family as much as we provided for him. Therefore we really should just remain open-minded and be prepared for anything that the future holds for us.

18

The Final Chapter

Twenty third December felt like the beginning of the end. We had been through a series of meetings and conversations with a number of professionals, including an independent reviewing officer whose job was to make an independent standards of care assessment of our suitability as foster carers. This was instructed by the Local Authority Designated Officer, LADO, and our agency completed the instruction. Two days before Christmas, we were served with what we now know is a recommendation of de-registration. The report was long and covered a lot of basis for fostering, which we accept and welcome. We do, however, appreciate that in three years it's never been as thorough as this! The independent reviewing officer, IRO, took everything apart and delivered it in a very detailed report, not only about the last year but a report on the past three years. It was brutal, it was detailed. I am a believer in that if you look hard enough for some things you will always find something. They looked too hard, and they looked for detail that didn't exist. They looked for reports from three years ago that actually were dealt with at the time. Lucas threw a photo of his mum at me and told me I was a dickhead. It didn't mean I had a dick on my forehead or that his mug needed to be thrown out of a window too, but that's what happened. Does that mean I failed in my care for him or was it just another day of being a parent, a professional parent at that. Our days of being a parent are filled with challenges and issues. If you cross analysed any parent, you will find days that didn't meet the exacting standards of the Social Services team.

I remember handing Lucas an L98A1 Cadet single shot, gas operated rifle, loosely based on the Army's SA80. This day in August was a week before he was removed from my care. Handing him that weapon was possibly the most dangerous thing I've ever done with Lucas. To an outsider reading this information on paper, they would consider it a rather dangerous and crazy thing to do. Teenagers with machine guns isn't everyone's idea of safe. When taken in context, it's relatively normal for me. I'm a qualified Skill At Arms Instructor and it was during a training camp with the cadets. The weapons were made safe, and I was surrounded by people like me doing what we do. It was just another thing in our life that continued beyond the realms of what other people thought would be safe or risky. Was it one hundred per cent risk free? No. However, we have enough safety measures to ensure that the risks are minimised, and safety precautions are in place to protect everyone.

Two days before Christmas, we received the first report. Two days before my entire family descended on our home to spend Christmas with us. Two days before the day I had applied for an overnight exemption for Lucas to stay with us, which was denied. It was a difficult Christmas I can assure you. Without delay, finally they sped up. Two days before New Year's Eve, we received the second report. Twenty nineth January, the annual review report compiled by our previous SSW, Noah, who loved us, and the new SSW, who we felt hated us, came through. It was not good.

There is a certain feeling of anxiety, adrenaline, and fear that you associate with metaphorically going to war. We have felt that we have been at war this entire time. The feeling of being unsupported, although not totally true, is still a feeling because we always thought it was too little too late. As we approached 2022, we felt like we were coming to our eleventh hour peace treaty. The war may be over soon. We lost. That's okay with us. We had forty-eight hours to come to terms with that before we needed to host the biggest party of the year at the hotel. We had to dress up, smile, laugh, and pour champagne to grateful hotel guests. It was one of the hardest shifts I've ever worked. I had to cook the evening meal, then jump into a suit and regale patrons with quick wit and banter to ensure they enjoyed their special night. I would break into a stream of tears and emotional breakdown whilst facing a corner or window. Quickly catching myself, drying my eyes, and delivering that fake smile and laugh that I had worked so hard on being realistic. Some people saw through it, some didn't. If they did, they respectfully didn't acknowledge it. Inside, I was having the worst night of my life, thinking of the decisions over and over again. Trying to process what life was going to be like next without helping young people achieve their goals. Especially the boys I had grown close to, Lucas and William. Life without them and, for them, life without us. It was a despairing evening.

Shortly after the new year celebrations, Robin and I disappeared for a couple of weeks, leaving the dog to manage the hotel. It was a much-needed rest physically. Mentally, the trauma continued. We had our instruction to attend a new panel meeting whilst we were away. We responded dutifully. Robin was less impressed and told them he was too emotionally drained to continue. I wasn't going to give up so would hold the torch for both of us. I understand why he didn't want to do it any more. He felt like he knew the outcome and thought, 'What's the point?' I don't blame him. I also agreed with him, but I had told Lucas that we would do everything we could to get him home. I wasn't going to fall at the last hurdle. I would carry Robin through the finish line.

The panel came and went. The outcome we knew was coming came. There was a distant hope that perhaps the panel of professionals would see through all the haze created by the allegation and see us for who we really are. This was followed two weeks later by the decision letter to formalise the decision to de-register. It came at the same time as the local authority for Lucas also confirming they wouldn't support any residency orders due to the outcome of the internal investigations of our agency. Bad news always comes in threes, so it wasn't a surprise to find the Army Cadet Force followed suit. Due to the outcome of the internal investigations of the agency, they couldn't support my continued employment working with children. Surprisingly, I wasn't as angry as I had been in the past. I had managed to suppress my emotions to such a level that I was now immune to this kind of bad news. It wouldn't, however, be as easy for Lucas. That would be hard. The next day, we put the house up for sale, realising our big home, built to house a gaggle of foster kids, was no longer needed. We realised that Lucas was never coming home and our future as carers was over. We pondered over the ideas of where our life would take us next. It was a difficult thing to think about. We had spent fifteen years becoming dads, and now it was all over. We feel more for Lucas than anyone else. He had spent nearly three years in our care and we involved him in our family so much because he was always told he was on a permanent placement with us. To be told that was over must have been awful for him and we only wish it could be different. We realised that the system suffers zero-risk bias and looking for corroboration in investigations only leads to loss for everyone involved. The agency that invested thousands in training and development, the kids, and the circle of influence around us, including charities and future possibilities, not to mention yours truly. All the people negatively impacted by the accusation of one person is truly astounding, beyond the ability of rational comprehension.

This book has been my therapy to myself, a journey that has been fraught with challenges and, as my neighbours put it, 'never a dull day in the borough'. I think the therapy of writing helps us all, like writing an angry email to someone and deleting it before you send it. I'm hoping that there are other couples out there who take the learnings from my experience, which in turn may actually help them start the journey to be awesome carers, whether they are single sex or not. Perhaps it's for others to understand the rarely understood world of foster care and 'the system'. The story of what it's like being a foster carer and that single sex foster carers aren't that evil, despite what the police think. I hope whoever reads the book learns, or understands, something more than they did when they started reading. I certainly have taken a lot of wonderful lessons from the books on fostering. I have read 'Nurturing Attachments' by Kim Golding three times. I love 'Raising Boys' by Steve Biddulph too. It's funny and resonates with us quite closely. Although 'The Book You Wish Your Parents Had Read (and Your Children Will Be Glad That You Did)' by Phillipa Perry was a difficult start, it was a fantastic read. I hope that one day 'Straight Dad, Gay Dad' is on some people's must-read list.

All I have ever wanted to do in life is to be of service, helping people – with either hospitality or charity or fostering. Now we know that Lucas is not coming home, or any other children for that matter. It is heart-breaking to know the system seems to be, by design, its own failing. I feel for all the children in care that haven't been afforded successful placements for one reason or another. It breaks my heart to think about Lucas and William and the life they could have had.